# TRUTH IS MORE SACRED

*a critical exchange on modern literature*

*a critical exchange on modern literature:*

James Joyce

D. H. Lawrence

Henry James

Robert Graves

T. S. Eliot

Ezra Pound

# TRUTH IS MORE SACRED

by EDWARD DAHLBERG and HERBERT READ

HORIZON PRESS          NEW YORK

© Edward Dahlberg and Sir Herbert Read
Library of Congress Catalog Card Number: 61–8514
Manufactured in the United States of America

# CONTENTS

on JAMES JOYCE

## *on* JAMES JOYCE: 1

DEAR HERBERT:

It is my fear that in this century of woe and panic literature may pass away, and that after the terrible hecatombs to come, it will be harder to find good books than the body of Osiris. These letters to you are poor oblations to the Muses, for like the Athenian women sacrificing at the tomb of Tereus, I offer you gravel instead of barley groats.

Your *Annals of Innocence and Experience* are lovely bucolics, and your sylvan notes are quiet, whereas I am rough and feral, and am likely to bite the tradesmen of letters. Dryden owned that he could censure bad works more easily than he could praise good ones; no matter, I prefer a virile negation to a comfortable, flaccid yea.

I abhor venal authors as well as the poet who is solely concerned with his dithyrambs and iambics, and who gives all his thoughts to words, without thinking about justice, affection and hope. His verses are the stibium pot of the harlot, or the hair-dye of the Colchian Medea. Though the external work be as white as the marble sepulchre, it is corrupt within. Sokrates prayed to Pan

11

asking that the inward and the outward man be one. Poetry today has been sacked by pleasure and novelty just as Troy was by Helen. In the English *Spectator* it is asked: "Who is the better for beholding the most beautiful Venus?" I regard James Joyce, Andre Gide, Cocteau, Rimbaud, Verlaine, Eliot, Pound, as the bawds in the beauty parlor on Mount Ida. They worship the manes of Oscar Wilde. However, it is my purpose to give a caveat to the raw apprentices of beauty.

There are many reasons for our task; there is a good deal of the eavesdropping criticism of Polonius on present-day literature; Polonius will never praise an audacious book by an obscure poet, except behind the arras, nor will he attack a renowned bad poet. If one assails a famous malefactor of the beauty-arts he not only incurs his venom, but raises up a sodality of foes. There is also the bodkin of the poltroon, Silence: he won't bury a volume in open battle or in the whoring book-review columns, but shuffles the book into limbo by not mentioning it. The tyranny of Silence has brought about a censorship of books. "The discouragement of all learning, the stop of Truth" we attribute to countries where dictators proscribe what intellectual victuals are pernicious to the entrails of the State. When Pope wrote the *Dunciad*, those, whose books he stabbed to death, answered him, and some with valor. Dr. Johnson says that to attack a stupid book is a benefaction to the nation; if the writer goes unpunished, he will harm the race of bards, and murder a whole century. But these are pusillanimous times, and most authors are more concerned with selling wind to noddles than in going to Golgotha which is suffering for meditation and truth.

We live in the heyday of the liar; there is scarce a man who utters the word, honest, who is not a skulker, or one who sighs for candor who is not Iago. The only way to return to wisdom, to Plato, Aristotle, Solon, Erasmus, Linnaeus, is to expunge from the lexicon the words honest, genius, art, and beauty.

Many readers go to critics with a simple heart, hoping to find out what authors are not quacks, or which books will enliven their identity; they quit acquiring a few hard terms, such as brachylogies, eikonologies, solecisms. Though their conceits are more stuffed than they were before, they are still committed to read the same squab grammarians and poetasters.

I cannot tell anyone how to write well, and aside from asserting that the god Thoth invented vowels and semivowels, I have no grammatical knowledge. Philo Judaeus spoke of those who grew gray in grammar, and Clement of Alexandria had no patience with those who chattered like turtle-doves about punctuation and syntax. The grammarians are always boys. If the language of the author does not smell of the mountains, the forest ash, or the rude hearth, the poem is wicked. There is no good verse that does not make the reader stronger in intellect, and which does not give him legs and arms he did not have before. The *Iliads* enlarges the mind, and strengthens the will no less than the river Skamander, or Mount Taurus. A truthful book is in the best of health. When Sokrates was making ready to take the hemlock, he asked his friend Crito to sacrifice a cock to Aesculapius, the god who gave him the vigor to discourse on wisdom in the agora. For Hermes, god of speech and messenger of death, guides the poet, and he, whose words are laden with some moiety of the Kosmos, also breathes forth a brave destiny and death.

A book is a battle of the soul, and not a war of words. The art of logomachy is a useless one, and those who indulge in it are a mischievous brood. They know what is sometimes pleasant, but seldom important. Suppose we inform our readers that Anaxagoras of Clazomenae was the first Greek to publish a book, that Lasus invented the dithyramb, Stesichorus of Himera, the hymns, and that Alcman the Spartan furnished us with the choral, and Anacreon the amorous song; will this do any more than to give us airs and lard our pride. True knowledge purges the intellect better than hyssop. Nobody can write an immaculate book, save an empty person, just as no one is ever virtuous, except unexpectedly; for the right idea rises up from the soul as suddenly as Hermes when he brings lamentations to men. Only a coxcomb is positive that his next book will be a masterpiece: "A shallow mind thinks his writings divine; a man of sense imagines he writes tolerably well," says La Bruyère.

Everything is a surprise to man; if he writes badly he is astounded, or, well, amazed; when he says something virtuous, he is delirious. He must be on guard every instant of his life not to be an evil person, and then not to invent verses which engender more witlings and dunderheads than there are already in the world.

What our age lacks most of all is sense and health. There can be no just words well arranged without vigor. "I swear upon my virility," testifies François Villon. That a great deal of modern verse is senseless, and belongs in the spital-house, only an enervated fool will deny. Few are strong enough to eschew a diseased book. Plato tells of a certain Leontius who knew that there were some corpses on the outside of the wall, which he wanted very much to see although he knew he would be disgusted if he looked at them. Unable to resist his impulse, he ran up to the cadavers, saying to his eyes, "Take your fill, ye wretches, of the fair sight."

The longing to be mad or ignorant is the delirium of the multitude, and it is as strong in men as the craving in swine for dirt, or in mullets for turbid water. To spend one's life in the sty without books is the misery in Erebus. Next to a friend who provides the heart with the honey in Hymetus, no less than a steadfast wife, is a wise poet who is the only cure there is for having to be in this world. Literature empowers the spirit; the *Iliads* is bread and patience no less than Noah. We wander everywhere in our souls to gather ourselves up for death and a good epitaph, and there is little rest save in a book which is like that unwrought stone which relieved Orestes of his madness when he sat on it.

Send me to the home for Ishmaels, or to Bedlam, where

Christopher Smart composed "Rejoice in the Lamb," and I am not ill, or insane, or niggard, but deprive me of the *Iliads,* or *The Compleat Angler,* or Blake's *Jerusalem,* and I am the ululant brute in the wilderness.

A sage is the strength of the people, and wise words are the gudgeons and the loaves of the nation, but they are more than the raiment and the meat for the flesh. A poet, who is not simply belly and pudendum, wants to instruct others; he himself is a suppliant, begging alms of the Kosmos, who is our Father, our Bread, and our Health. Who can be impervious to such precepts as Anarchasis offers us: "My covering is a cloak; my supper, milk and cheese."

Literature is about what is innocent and first. It is a doxology of heroes and localities; the *Iliads* is the catalogue of maritime towns and ships, Messe's towers for doves, and Tryon near Alphaeus's flood. For Ptolemy, virgin America on his map was Albion. Hermes, who gives us intimations of death, wears white raiment. When the commonalty is vigorous, the people remember their sacred origins. Homer tells us that Protesilaus was the first Greek to leap from his trireme and land at Troy. Pausanias admits that he saw the lump of mud which Prometheus used to mould original man. Protogenia, according to the Hellenes, was the primal woman. This interest in what you, Herbert, call the Annals of Innocence, is the energy of the polity. What man did at first makes for a literature of giants. Our search for beginnings exhales energies and oracles. Memory, or Mnemosyne, is chaste. Many of the poets know very little about the fathers who settled their homeland; some deserted their country, like Henry James, T. S. Eliot, and Ezra Pound.

The lotus-eaters are bestial because what they fear most is knowledge; they cower before the vast archives of ancient wisdom, and shun the graves of Apis and the headstone of Poseidon; their minds are too timorous to invent a colossus. The piety of Homer for the earliest fables is shown by his use of obsolete words. He preferred the old names for Chaeronea and Lebadea, and called the Nile by its archaic appellation, the River Egypt. His whole life was such a legend that it was told that his father was the river Meles. We are either Pigmies by the river Strymon who are overcome by cranes, or we are Titans. Man creates legends to avoid having a mean fate; Linnaeus adopted a nomenclature for his plants and insects derived from mythical Greek characters.

The spirit stinks when it is feeble, and it is no different with amorous exercises, for Aphrodite is surnamed Praxis which means action. Mnemosyne dilates the soul, for the spirit is either filled by memory or is unclean. Forgetting is one of the marvelous pleasures of man, and it equals his delight in being gross. Homer never wrote personal memoirs, like the novels of Flaubert, Proust, Lawrence, James, Joyce. This is an occupation for the lagging ear, and for the garrulous mind, and not for a potent intellect.

17

Man is either epic, or hates the sublime; he invents chimerae, harpies, eponymous giants, or he is scatophagous. Baudelaire said that the pothouse men of letters dote on excrements, which is the gallic salt of the novel. The *Ulysses* of James Joyce is the story of the scatological sybarites of the business world; it is a twenty-four hours' journey through ordure; a street-urchin's odyssey of a doddering phallus. James Joyce did in his novel what every business man craves to do, to be an epicure in the toilet. Has not the bourgeoisie relinquished every vision for the water-closet? Swift had far more learning than Joyce, which was not considerable, but he had passion and character. Still, *Gulliver's Travels* barely escapes being a tract on the Lilliputian revulsions that attack men without powerful minds and beliefs. Were it not for the legendary horse-people, the Houyhnhnms, *Gulliver's Travels* would have failed, and I think Dr. Johnson thought it did, for he pays much heed to Swift's life but gives only a laconic page to the *Travels*.

Joyce's *Ulysses* is the novel of epic cowardice; I do not blame him for divulging all the vices of men but for reducing them to unheroic dimensions. We must call wrath, dirt, lust, drunkenness—Agamemnon, Thersites, Ajax, Nestor, or sink the giants into little everyday characters. If the bad smells and ugly habits of men are the principal obsessions of the author, he has to translate them into Yahoos or Brobdingnags. Books are as ill as their authors, and often more so. Swift was sorely pained because men defecated and had evil odors. Both Pope and Swift, who were not scholars, showed an unusual interest in the vile. It is worth observing how far genius can go without great learning.

No poet can cocker his faults on the public pages of a book; he has to make them look a little like Cato or that Roman Curius who preferred his garden of turnips to gold. Poets are a profligate lot, and many a reader has been enervated and ravished by a book. Pope, born feeble, lived to be weaker; he had the body of a dwarf, but the fierce lusts of a burly Ajax. Richard Savage disappeared for weeks to drink and carouse with trulls in secret places outside London. Though Pope and Savage practiced the vices of Faustina, their verses show the visage of Marcus Aurelius. It is not my purpose to judge the lives of the poets, for they are vain all day long and more amorous than a quail or partridge.

Pallas Athene signifies wisdom and war, and the olive which is sacred to that goddess represents peace but not ignominious submission. Wisdom has to be fought for with the same valor that the Greeks defended Thermopylae, and the javelin, the pike, the spear of Pelian ash are study, fortitude, and chagrin. The image of Minerva which Diomede and Ulysses carried away from Troy was made of the bones of Pelops, but a savage art is better than an effeminate one. The slovens of the muses are like that Greek who was so lazy that he had never

dropped his hand as far as his navel. They are the enemies of Minerva and Aphrodite, both of whom are god-
desses of action.

Joyce adopts the ancient hero, Ulysses, as the title of
his novel, though his men of Dublin are not demigods
but everyday gnomes with watery volitions. All that
comes out of a man's mouth is not wise or reasonable;
were it so we would be Aristotle all day long. But words,
when not governed, are a symptom of velleity in the
author. Dedalus, his principal thinker, is the architect
in Greek myth, but who can imagine that this shadow of
torpor was constructed by Daedalus. It cannot be claimed
either that a ledgerbook of legendary names can add to
our understanding. Aphrodite, Artemis, Nereus, Isis are
the inward elements of our passions; we mould them in
our blood as the ashes of Prytaneum were kneaded
in the holy waters of the Alpheus.

No one can exercise his faculties by reading a simple
list of the appellations of the gods, nor is it original to
turn two diverse words into one, giving it double organs.
Who cares to exhaust his brain searching for a verb
which has wandered away from the substantive, or look
for a noun that has been abducted by Pluto, or was never
born? What reason is there for trying to make an adjective behave like a male verb? These eunuchal adjectives
sigh forth their concupiscence but are unable to perform
their duties as verbs to the sentence. There is a labial
failure in *Ulysses* similar to the confusion of tongues of
the people in the plains of Shinar; the noises in the belly

and the rasping and hawking of the throat take the place of the alphabet. Besides, his words are lubricious, and a book ought not to send men to the brothel, especially in my country, where there is much vice, but so hard to acquire if one is poor or modest. The houses of Venus are either in the hands of Plutus or hidden in Tartarus. There are few prostitutes for the commons. What we need in America are more chaste books and more whore-houses. The poor you will always have with you, says Christ, and prostitution is always necessary, declared Tolstoy.

My dear Herbert, I regard this epistle as plain book husbandry; first of all reading is a purificatory rite, and as your own muse pacifies my nature let me then hear from you the songs of your native England. Coleridge, as you so well know, having written with such compassion of his miseries, was a great but wretched nature, and it was Charles Lamb who told him that if he would read *The Compleat Angler* he would be quieter.

## *on* JAMES JOYCE: 2

DEAR EDWARD:

When I read your letter I do not think of you as a feral beast, ready to bite the tradesmen of letters, but rather as a druid, still hiding in the desecrated grove, hissing his imprecations into the dusty track of the marauders. I should say, perhaps, that such is the image I would rather have of you, for it is a just image; whereas these poor tradesmen of letters, whom you so justly. despise for their ignorance or corruption, are fellow priests who have fallen by the way. I have made you a druid on purpose—you might have preferred to be a poet in Troy. That would serve as well, for my point is that the real enemies of literature and art today are not our corrupted brothers, but the forces that corrupt them—the whole of the hideous, heartless civilization in which we are involved. Like the Druids and the Trojans, we are about to be exterminated by "ignorant armies." Naturally I don't refer to Russian armies or American armies, though they can now obliterate the human race should the fancy take them. I refer most literally to the armies of ignorance, to the rootless proletariat that is the Great Horde bearing down on our slender temples. They are armed with the most terrible of weapons: indifference. If they were conscious enemies, it would not be so bad. An enemy is at least obliged to have an intelligence service —*some* of them would have to read our books! But no: they read only their pulp, their printed mash of sadism and eroticism. The rest they trample under their heavy boots.

There are two points I am trying to make: one is that we must recognize the true enemies of art, who are not a few cowards in our own ranks, but the barbarians outside the gates. But then art has always had its enemies, and the second point that I shall try to establish is that the enemies of our own time are peculiarly insidious.

Let me take the second point first. Burckhardt has a warning for us. In his *Reflections on History*, a fund of wisdom on these questions, he writes:

> When the man of culture sits down to the banquet of the art and the poetry of past times, he will not be able, or wish, to resist the lovely illusion that these men were *happy* when they created their great works. Yet all they did was to rescue the ideals of their time at the cost of great sacrifice, and wage in their daily life the battle we all fight. It is only to us that their creations look like youth rescued and perpetuated.

You will admit the general truth of that statement. All the same, Burckhardt himself has given us plenty of rea-

sons for regarding our own age as peculiarly and fatally
barbarous—it is that combination of democracy and
money-making which has perverted socialism itself, and
turned the world into one vast comfort-seeking bourgeoisie. Already in 1870 Burckhardt saw that the dominating feeling of the age had become "the desire of the
masses for a higher standard of living," a perfectly
"reasonable" desire, but one that has nothing to do with
greatness or glory.

Suppose for a moment that the masses could be
offered this choice: in return for a 10% lowering in the
standard of living, you can have another Shakespeare—
do you think (provided they could understand the terms
in which the choice must be expressed) that for a moment they would hesitate? Have I made the price too
high? Make it 1% and still they would shake their massive wooden head.

My only object in making this point is to reduce to its
true proportions your attack on certain of our contemporaries. In your letter you concentrate on Joyce. Well,
Joyce was my adolescent pabulum; I imbibed him in
monthly doses, as he appeared in *The Egoist* and *The
Little Review*. The early books influenced me, especially
*The Portrait of the Artist as a Young Man* (the very
food of adolescence!). But as I matured I grew tired of
the diet, and no doubt its substance was changing. For
whatever reason, I never committed myself enthusias-
tically to either *Ulysses* or *Finnegans Wake* (their ob-
scurities seemed to me to be masks for sentimentality). I

therefore have no retractions to make now, but at the same time I find your characterization of *Ulysses* too unjust. Scatological it is, and finally one is disgusted; but "a twenty-four hours' journey through ordure"? Only ordure? Surely there is a light reflected from the sea in the opening chapter; and in spite of word-making that may now sound intolerably artificial, there are rhythms and cadences of astonishing beauty. It has been praised for its structure ("il suit la grande ligne de *l'Odyssée*," said our polyglot friend Ezra at the time), but who cares for a form so studiously disguised? I prefer the form of *Tristram Shandy*! (Do not mistake me—I am not against form in fiction, but it must be taut and dramatic, clearly discernible; of such form perhaps only Henry James is a master). Again, *Ulysses* has been praised for its realism, but as you say, it only succeeds in reducing the vices of men to unheroic dimensions. Yes: a sick book, but a significant one. A sick book for a sick age. We must struggle for health, you say—sense and health. But we must also diagnose our sickness. And that sickness is not literary: it is social.

I have no wish to deflect your blows, but I do not think venality is the common characteristic of the authors you mention—I doubt if the seven you mention have *any* characteristic in common. Indeed, I find your list very confusing, for what (except perversion!) has Gide in common with Verlaine, or Cocteau with Rimbaud? I do not think we need discuss Gide and Cocteau in this connection, but all the others have written authentic poetry.

You say that literature is about what is "innocent and first." What could be more innocent than "la chanson bien douce" of Verlaine?

> Le ciel est, par-dessus le toit,
>     Si bleu, si calme!
> Un arbre, par-dessus le toit,
>     Berce sa palme.
>
> La cloche, dans le ciel qu'on voit,
>     Doucement tinte.
> Un oiseau sur l'arbre qu'on voit
>     Chante sa plainte . . .

It is true that Verlaine was anything but innocent in his life, but I suspect that you are judging the man and not his work—the worst critical sin. Verlaine himself regretted his lost innocence—even in this very poem I have quoted:

> —Qu'as-tu fait, ô toi que voilà
>     Pleurant sans cesse,
> Dis, qu'as-tu fait, toi que voilà,
>     De ta jeunesse?

As for Rimbaud, he may not have been innocent, even in his poetry, but where will you find such another poet who saw things "first"? He even wrote a poem on this very subject—"Les poëtes de sept ans." And what is "Le bateau ivre" but a long chain of things first seen, of things seen in their primal innocency? But I suspect we use the word innocence in very different senses. For me it is a question of pure sensation, of uncorrupted *vision*. In your use of the word (and elsewhere of the word "health") I seem to detect ethical overtones. You seem to be calling on the poet to purify men's hearts. I would say that that is the business of the priest or the philosopher, and that it is the poet's business to purify their eyes. We cannot feel aright unless we see aright. The whole function of art is cathartic, not didactic. One might even say, with Confucius and Dante, that poetry is a purifying process, an effort to keep the language clean, to avoid distortion of meaning. But before the word can be exact, the vision must be clear. That is what T. E. Hulme insisted on so strongly, and I think our poets have been good poets to the degree that they have followed his advice. "The test for poetry is the range of pleasure it affords as sight, sound, and intellection"— that is our friend Zukofsky's measuring-rod, and I know of no better, and you will see he places sight first. It is a test that rightly leaves Homer and Shakespeare the first of poets, and yet plays havoc with our fashionable reputations. Yet it has in it nothing of moral judgment. Do not place too much reliance on the word "intellection," for I think Zukofsky means no more by it than the lively movement of the mind.

In revulsion against our complex mechanical civilization, you yearn for the primitive furniture of the *Iliad*. You might as well cry for the moon, or some remoter satellite. I agree that great literature has been "a doxol-

ogy of heroes and localities," but we must not look for
our heroes in unexpected places, and Brooklyn Bridge is
perhaps as good a locality as Troy—as Hart Crane
proved imperfectly. It is the purity of vision that matters, and not the shape or location of the thing seen.
There are even modern heroes, but poetry does not celebrate them. Doughty was probably the last poet to write
of heroes, but he had to return to primitive times. Is it
that we suspect our heroes? Can you conceive the possibility of a good poem on the heroic Gandhi? The last
heroic poem in the tradition of the *Iliad* celebrated the
poet himself—it was Wordsworth's *Prelude*.

We are inevitably age-bound, not merely subject to
the *Zeitgeist*, but drawing our sustenance from a com-
post which we inherit, a seedbed which is universal.
There are certain states which we cannot accomplish,
because we have too much knowledge, or too much self-
consciousness. Objectivity is one of them. The modern
poet cannot depict the hero because he inevitably con-
fuses himself with the hero. We see everything through
our own subjectivity. We talk about the anonymity of
Homer or Shakespeare, but we mean their objectivity.
They see their heroes with exactly the same innocent eyes
that they see a ship or a mountain. Admittedly Shakespeare stands at the border-line, but the attempt to iden-
tify Shakespeare with one of his heroes will never suc-
ceed. If he is Hamlet, how can he be Lear or Prospero?
Shakespeare is identical with all his heroes, which means
that he is no one of them. Joyce was well aware of this

problem, and he was great to the extent that he escaped from his subjectivity. But he did not escape, for he identified himself with Stephen Dedalus, and as you say, converted his demigods into gnomes.

The rarest thing in history, said Burckhardt, is greatness of soul. The rarest thing in literature is objectivity, and perhaps this is also a characteristic of greatness of soul. Burckhardt said that the latter "resides in the power to forego benefits in the name of morality, in voluntary self-denial, not merely from motives of prudence but from goodness of heart." There is a similar self-denial in the great poet, and a similar goodness of heart; but he must forego the benefits of success in the name of truth. And this, as you say, is the heyday of the liar. But truth, too, is a word to expunge from the lexicon, for it is in the name of truth that the biggest crimes are now committed. That is why I think it is better to insist on the image, on the icon, on the vision that has not yet been smeared with unctuous morality.

## *on* JAMES JOYCE: 3

DEAR HERBERT:

It may take a century to clean out the Augean stables of literature; this is not the labor of the Lydian Hercules, who wore the scarlet apron of Omphale, but the work of the decrepit Hercules of Gaul who had a crumpt back and a tawny skin. We despise the old because we prefer to be novel rather than wise. Lucian remarks that the Hercules Ogmius tied the ears of his listeners to his own tongue; unless the ears are yoked to a just tongue they are a pair of lying, sottish porkers. I am very glad that you cite Louis Zukofsky who insists that the mind must govern the ear. Otherwise, books and poems are a rammish Babel of brutal sounds which confuse men.

Herbert, I cannot pity the sick, venal Cains of literature, from whom Conscience, fearful of being killed, has fled. These dunces wail for Melville, Thoreau, Whitman, while lurking in the thickets, waiting to ambush a brave book and throw it into the ditch of Limbo. Every ragged Ishmael of the Muses is their prey, and a woeful reminder to them that what they are winnowing is not

Chaldean wheat but chaff. As Pope has it, "Still Dunce the second reigns like Dunce the first." Pope wrote: "Some neither can for wits or criticks pass, as heavy mules are neither horse, nor ass."

Milton said in the *Areopagitica* that anyone who kills a book is a gallowsbird, and a murderer. He who inters the poets and thinkers of a nation beatifies the rabble. No people, declared Ruskin, can last which has made a mob of itself. Do not slain poems cry out as piteously as Abel's blood? Am I to forgive book-guillotinists and plagiaries who creep into another man's volume as the Hermit-crab houses itself in a dead mollusk's shell?

There is rust and moth in the social corpus; the books are no less suppurated than the flesh of Job. We can pardon those who smite us because they have spleen, or their portion is rags and neglect, but what will you do, O friend, with the fox and the weasel? Shall a writer lie and spew forth such words as the mole and the bat cannot abide, and be comforted for it? St. Augustine remarked that even Catiline did not love his own villainies, but I think that Cyclops cared only to be lawless. One does not go to a book to acquire a new malady, and I don't think, Herbert, that a writer is a polypus who assumes the color of the rock to which it fastens itself. There is such a great dearth of integrity among authors that even an honest writer without talent is a genius.

Negation is the health of vision, and the enquiring and ransacking Elenchus was the denying genius of Sokrates, but to curse the ground, and to stare with indifferent eyes at the Ocean is wicked. It is corrupt to detest CREATION, and what philosopher or poet can hate the Kosmos, and MAKE a book?

I take great pains not to find errors in a wise author, or make little of them. I am of your bent of mind when you write: "I have no wish to decry the great intelligence, the general felicity and immense achievement of Milton." However, James Joyce has been called a gigantic Iapetus by critics. Had his flagitious phrases the hardness of those precious stones in Paradise, I should be astonished, as evil has magnitude and luminosity; Lucifer is a fallen star.

*Ulysses* is the inkpot of our age of slovens, and the shibboleth of the sham Gideon is that a book must represent its times. This is a sick screed, for who wants to be as pitiless, debauched, and insane as our century? We have killed the grass, the marigolds, and in place of the heifer the auto lows, and instead of the horse, machines neigh in our heads. *Ulysses* does not cure the nervous, the thwarted, and the fallen, but relieves them of all hope. Prometheus, though his liver is gnawed every day, which is suffering contemplation, grows a new liver again every night that provides him with intellectual strength.

Do not think that I regard James Joyce as one of the companions of Swift or the ancients. There is no way I know of to write about an inferior author without sinking one's self except by comparing him with the seers

of literature. The river Alphaeus was said to have min-
gled with a lissomy fountain, and this is a wedding
hymn, or one of those phallic songs from which, as Aristotle said, Attic comedy originated. One, however, who
strokes a Chimaera or a Briareus will carry away the
smell and the deformity of both.

You maintain, Herbert, that you see no affinity between Joyce and Gide. As to their diction I am in no
position to argue against you. Gide said nothing rather
amiably, whereas Joyce was far less the master of nulli-
ties. However, Oscar Wilde was the idol, Baal, for each
of them. There is a Heliogabalus in many men, and some
say in all, and it is idle to discount the influence of
Wilde. Were it otherwise, we would still be observing
the rites of Hymen, and smearing marjoram on the gate-
posts of Amaryllis.

Poets suffer from debility more than other men, having worn themselves out for truth and fame, the first having no chance in the world without the help of that
pander reputation. Pope could not stand on his feet
without the support of very tight stays, but his language
was manly. Swift ran up and down a hill several times a
day to overcome giddiness which was in time to turn his
faculties to unhearing stone, but he wrote in the masculine gender. James Joyce was a grammar gabbler more
fit for chasing the geese of Camelot than for literature.
His will, which is the adamant nerve of the intellect,
was so desiccated that he could seldom proceed from

the noun to the verb. I borrow, Herbert, your quotation from Addison who said of another writer, our language sunk under him.

The clodpates of all factions wallow in the most purulent vernacular. Poor Penny Judgment of polite literature has no more sense than Better Social Feelings, both imagining that every brand-new word minted by the voracious philisters of trade must be included in the modern lexicon to show that they are familiars of the times. The consequence is that servile neologisms, invented by Dr. Greed, are the language of the oppressed classes. Slavish words are far more potent than political alterations, and scribblers who draw their metaphors and barbarisms from avaricious merchants can no longer understand the curative English of Chaucer, Gower, Addison and Dryden. There is such a great scarcity of country English nowadays that Dr. Small Knowledge of our academies of learned nonsense is ignorant of centaury, fenugreek or drupe. He cannot comprehend the Gospels written for poor fishermen, vinedressers, and husbandmen, because the parables of Christ are derived from the ploughshare, the weir, and the orchard. The misuse of words induces evil in the soul, said Sokrates.

Joyce cowardly submits to every evil imagining in his heart, always degrading a meditative line for the sake of a scurrile pun, or parody. He writes that when the Jews entered the wilderness they desired to build an altar to Jehovah, but that when the Romans came into the country ruled by Saturn, they said, "Let us construct a water-

34

closet." To say this is hardly in accord with the annals of Livy, or the *Aeneid,* would appear supererogatory, were it not easy to gull the ignorant, and to amuse trifling noddles.

James Joyce wrote a canting, riff-raff English; whenever he was about to be serious he could not be contemplative because he thought it more important to be humorous. He relinquished the heroic to draw a simper from the reader. "To utter a mere jest ornately is like beautifying an ape," one ancient rhetor asserted. "Lawn Tennyson" is a facetious phrase, and his reference to Priapus as "the limp father of thousands" is frolicsome; but who is ready to mew himself up in a novel of such tedious length for an occasional smile?

There is also, Herbert, the tragedy of separation; you have said in the *Phases of English Poetry* that the writer must find a communal alphabet. The poet is wild and savage, lost in the forests of Nôdh, and his verse is the private monologue of Cain, for our books are no longer our brother's keeper. The decline of a living English as we know it in Langland's *Piers Ploughman,* Chaucer, Waller, Izaak Walton, has been so great that there is no familiar tongue common to both the writer and the people. The unfettered cupidity of businessmen has led to a brutish gibberish and craven dialect. Jonathan Swift, inveighing against new words, said that the Struldbruggs of one age were unable to understand those of another, and predicted that after a hundred years there would be no conversation, and that they would live as strangers in their own country. Joyce, the modern Struldbrugg, writes: ". . . the odoriferous flambeaus of the paranymphs have escorted to the quadrupedal proscenium of connubial communion." ". . . in habit dun beseeming her megrims and wrinkled visage, nor did her hortative want of it effect for incontinently . . ." "Married to Bloom, to greaseaseabloom." "Knock at the door. Last tip to titivate. Cockcarracarra," and "Ventriloquise. My lips closed. Think in my stom. What?"

Once the pinchbeck novelties of language in *Ulysses* are dropped, Platitude is King. What has passed for an unusual assortment of words, and for originality, are neologisms, bombast, solecisms, and perverse and corrupt sequences of words. There is very little grammar in his sentences, for the author was so bent upon being new that he was seldom coherent. Driven by a hysteria to be artistic, he babbled, dropping caitiff puns, immolating any serious thoughts he had by gross alliteration: "Miss Douce of satin douced her arm away." "She smiled on him. But sister bronze outsmiled her." "She smiled-smirked supercillious."

The pedant milks every poem and novel for the grammar in them, and are such college gulls as to mistake musty inversions in diction for originality: "spluttered out of her mouth her tea," or "Tossed to fat lips his chalice." Never in English literature has language fallen into such dotage. The Homeric line has so much primal strength that it would appear that the Smyrna bard used the Pelian ash for a pen. Joyce, however, cannot father

a virile sentence, nor hurl the verb as Achilles does a
boulder; his comparisons are knavish and foolish.
Winckelmann spent hours murmuring the similes of
Homer to himself; the Houyhnhnms are also renowned
for the justness of their figures of speech.

Every line of Joyce suffers from asthmatic shortness
of breath or blank senility. As debilitated as a Lilliput,
he could not lift a preposition or adverb and set it down
where it belongs, and he was often too tired to wait for
the verb. "Mulch of dung. Best thing to clean ladies' kid
gloves," "A tiny coffin flashed by. In a hurry to bury. A
mourning coach." The banalities gravel the imagination; and his scurvy misuse of words is Scythian rapine:
"the first quick hot touch of his hand," "Whitehot passion was in that face, passion silent as the grave," "sky
. . . violet, color of Molly's new garters," "steam of
newbaked jampuffs rolypoly poured out from Harrison's," "swilling, wolfing gobfuls of sloppy food," "Professor MacHugh murmured softly, biscuitfully."

The plain speech of Bottom the Weaver was honest
and pithy enough to take care of the needs of a Spinoza,
as Louis Zukofsky has shown, but what gawk, jake, or
jolt-noddle said this: "Accordingly his first act was with
characteristic sangfroid to order these commodities
quietly."

The book is not rich evidence of manhood: "jingle
jaunty blazes boy," "jingle jaunty jaunty," "Encore!
Clapclipclap," "jimjam lickitup secretness," and "gush,
flow, joygush," would raise the eyes of Falstaff and his

roisterers in any jolly tavern. To the shades of Henry James Joyce here is: "Douce gave vent to a splendid yell, a full yell of full woman, delight, joy, indignation."

The comma and the circumflex have taken the place of a homely gnome, and subtle punctuation is more important than the water-cress, the leek, and the anise seed. The adjective is the Achilles' heel of the sentence; a line can be mortally wounded by a supernumerary epithet. One who uses the adjective as a male verb has no appreciation of energetic prose: "Hoarsely the apple of his throat hoarsed softly."

He had cormorant vulgarity, and an unappeasable appetite for a garbage-Minerva and Eros: "Sandwich. Ham and his descendants mustered and bred there," "She let free sudden in rebound her nipped elastic garter smack-warm against her smackable woman's thigh." The doggerel and commonplaces that do not make the reader skittish embowel him. Cato fell upon his sword; to expire by a pun is more malefic; banter, says La Bruyère, is often a sign of a want of intelligence. "Gulfer of souls, engulfer. Hesouls, shesouls, shoals of souls," "south mouth: womb tomb," "Boylan socks skyblue clocks," "quivery loveshivery," "eaten a bad egg. Poached eggs on ghost," "sunnywinking leaves," "His frocktails winked in bright sunshine," "looked up shybrightly." Can anybody applaud this apotheosis of nonsense? There are many reasons why a writer is a bore, but none of them will save him.

Vile words are an ineradicable damage to the soul,

and neither Orestes nor Oedipus suffer more from Nemesis than readers from the injuries wrought by these befouled ghosts that can never be quieted or sepulchred.

Joyce pined for the "larches, firs . . . and the trees of the conifer family," "the giant ash of Galway, and the elm of Kildare," which were fast dying out, but this is the weather of easy poesy. His brief sorrow for the "decayed raths and cromlechs and grianauns . . . the ruins of Clonmaconois, Cong Abbey, Glen Inaugh" is agreeable because the names are unfamiliar, and remote, but this is the pleasure rather than the sorrow of a monody. One can make little account of this dirge which is a negligible moiety of the novel. He seldom caresses our memories, or instructs our feelings; shortly after this he furnishes the reader with a brief list of the names of a few saints and martyrs, "Phocas of Sinope and S. Julian Hospitator . . . S. Simon Stylites . . . and S. John of God," without telling us what they felt, thought, or did. This is the kind of outside use of titles of books and names of thinkers, which mummify and grave the reader; for every good book is an awakener. Wyndham Lewis mentions the outside man in literature, but is himself one of the tragedies of the modern exterior man.

Joyce's recitation of sundry Dublin thoroughfares is a phlegmatic street-directory. An author does not ennoble the intellect by merely mentioning the sages or myths which are sacred to humanity. We do not quit a book with more understanding because the writer, like an Elizabethan crier with his lanthorn, bawls out, "Zeus,

Osiris, Mnevis, Apis, St. Thomas, Origen, Barabbas."

In Blake every cobblestone is an adage; the alleys of Hempstead are the bulls of Bashan, Piccadilly the Vale of Hinnom, and the lusts thereof are the body of Peor. For Christopher Smart a toad, spider, draper, fuller, vintner, are the arteries and the inly piping vines to his affections. Joyce writes, ". . . Blackrock, Kingstown and Dalkey, Clonskea, Rathgar," and Blake says, "Battersea and Chelsea mourn for Cambel and Gwendolen, Hackney and Holoway sicken for Estrid and Ignoge." A wise book is a brave and good epitaph.

## *on* JAMES JOYCE: 4

DEAR HERBERT:

You make a significant distinction in your noble little volume *Phases of English Poetry,* between passion and the senses. The books done by Olympian jackdaws reveal the exquisite sensibilities of the Moslem beggar who delicately removes the vermin from his clothes and tenderly puts them down on the ground. We gently stroke our worms, says Josephine Herbst, author of *The New Green World,* that tender gospel of American herbages. It does not matter whether words are the wild honey and locusts of St. John, or are as goatish as Rabelais'. What is important is that they should be hardy. A farm road, a glebe, a plain and an elm breed charity and pity, which the fiction of groundless city surfeit and nausea lacks.

Our books are imposthumes and portable hospitals, but is this a sign of feeling or of compassion for one human being? Lord Bacon said that we should not confound the delicacy of the nerves with extreme tenderness of the heart. You think, Herbert, that I go too far in speaking of *Ulysses* as the feculent droppings of the

Yahoos that sit upon the branches. Kierkegaard has written that genius is a sin; there is no doubt that Rabelais influenced Swift from whom Joyce purloined his spurious gusto to create one of the grossest sins in modern literature. The title, *Ulysses*, is false, for it is the little Iliad of everyday disgusts.

The Homeric Ulysses has intellectual powers, and so long as he is bent upon overcoming Neptune and Polyphemus, and avoiding the Sirens, he is a Titan, but after he returns to Penelope he falls into gluttony and aimless longevity.

There is one imperial theme in *Ulysses*, and that is the lament for the ancient patriarchy which has vanished. St. Augustine also believed that the human race was dwindling; Nimrod ranged the Plains of Shinar when behemoth lived, and the olden towns were founded by giants. According to the fables the size of men decreased as they grew civilized; the body of Orestes, found beneath the floor of a smithy, was said to be ten feet in height.

Joyce had not the strength for a tragedy in the groves of Baal. In the place of the Titans, Osiris, the solar prepuce, Thoth, the god of the alphabet, Father Belus, intellectual fire, we have the shades of Oscar Wilde, and that love of which no man dare speak.

Once we depart from elemental symbols and ritual the poet and the reader are hurt and gibbering minds in the meadows of Asphodel. Leopold Bloom is a gulligut Odysseus who comes home to Penelope and his porkers.

He has spent his force on Molly and a gallimaufry of Dublin trulls. Phallus is dead, and Leopold Bloom's seed is too weak to remain in the matrix of his wife for more than seven months. Homer said the child which Neptune begot upon the nymph was born a whole year after the conception. Rabelais, citing Aulus Gellius, asserts that this length of time was suitable to the majesty of Neptune. Gargantua was almost twelve months in the womb of Gargamella; Rudolph Bloom was an abortive birth. Joyce's modern genealogy is: "Moses begat Noah and Noah begat Eunuch." Rabelais, giving massive dimension to the progenitors of Gargantua and Pantagruel, writes: Hercules "begat Hapamouche," who showed men how to "dry neat's tongues in the chimney"; he begat Gayoffe, "whose ballocks were of poplar, who begat Grangousier, who begat Gargantua, who begat Pantagruel."

Bloom, a converted Protestant, is thrice removed from Abraham, Isaac, and Jacob, having been three times baptized. Since the death of his only son, Rudolph, Bloom has not gone into Molly, his wife, as Abraham went into Hagar. Bloom wears what Rabelais calls a hypocritical codpiece stuffed with wind; for Orpheus has not provided him with that great emerald which empowers the genital properties more than Alpha, Taurus, and the Mandrake root.

Patriarchy has gone, Jehovah, "the collector of prepuces" is no more; the pudendum of Osiris has been cast into the river Nile, and Leopold Bloom is a wittol. The

Jew in *Ulysses* is the phallus of the first fathers of man, Adam, Noah, and Jacob, the Performer, as Philo says his name signifies. Bloom is a Jew of the Diaspora. He is a hyphenate-Christian in Catholic Dublin, apart from his people, and from the Jahweh of the Kabala, who has august genitalia. "Are you not my dear son Leopold who left the house of his father and left the god of his fathers, Abraham and Jacob?"

A useful novel or poem is healed either by learning, myth or the use of hyperbole. A ribald book that is also contemplative is like those boxes of old in the shops of apothecaries called Silenuses, which Rabelais tells us had the "figures of satyres, bridled geese, saddled ducks, and harts on the outside to make people merry, but in which were kept balm, ambergris, musk, civet, and precious stones." Rabelais' book is the comedy of size. Feeding and laughter are vast, and Gargantua is himself a giant whose name was found on megalithic monuments. Gargantua has the sexual organs of an antediluvian mastodon, or those giants in the book of Enoch who were said to have the privy members of horses. Gulliver's travels to apocryphal lands is the allegory of distance. For remoteness of place is remarked, by Racine, to afford the same conveniences to a poet as length of time.

Swift, borrowing much from Rabelais, is much less successful, because Gulliver's hatred of man is diseased; it is far worse than Timon's misanthropy; the heart of the latter is wounded by man's savage ingratitude, but

44

the mind of Swift was tumored. Rabelais' words would be scurrile without the balm of learning, and affections, and were his attitude toward voiding and gendering contrary to the laws of nature. Swift finds man a mangy animal because he copulates and excretes; we admire his invention, and his remarkable nomenclature which comes out of the tragedy of size, showing that men are as small and as mean as a Lilliput, or as repulsive as the bulky Brobdingnags.

Swift could not cure his own imagination; almost at the end of Gulliver there is that cathartic Horse Gospel. He tried, with what valor no one may know, to extirpate from his mind those noisome images by limning a savory Horse People whose dung is inoffensive and who feed on a wisp of hay and oats. Swift lacked the affection of the sacred amorist whose pulses sigh when he hears, In the beginning was the Word. His reason was a dry, incontinent rage which no Antycyrian hellebore could purge. For Jonathan Swift the Kosmos was a carcase, which is blasphemous. He was dead to the ground of which we are made, and this is not a weak but an insane sin. Christopher Smart blessed the palmerworm, the weasel, the ossifrage, and a Lethophagus God. The late Eric Gill has spoken similarly, "Nature 'red in tooth and claw' is as much in accord with His will as small children singing hymns. Rocky mountains, grassy downs, rats, germs, and dung, all are things singing to us of Him."

The consequence of Swift's malady was an astonishing tract; the Dean was as relentless as Sisyphus; Joyce, however, suffered from an ailment too common in this age, the depravity of the will, which accounts for those perverted jests; he was unmanned by a pun.

*The Compleat Angler* can hinder a lickerish man for a time, which may save him from tedium and the waste of hope which demolishes the will. Not all can be content with Izaak Walton, or some only for a while. Those who seek other pleasures in literature, which life has denied them, should not be satisfied with a concupiscent book that has not the stone and character of Cato; such a volume is the shortest path to the lees of cloacal dreams.

A book should be as chaste as it is bawdy, which should enable one to understand Antisthenes when he exclaims, "I would rather go mad than feel pleasure." Homer himself detests venery as much as he is drawn by it, for he has Vulcan drop his seed on the thigh of Pallas Minerva, which is a fable the priapic acolytes of D. H. Lawrence, Cocteau, and Wilde never understood.

Walton says there are lustful and continent fish. Rabelais and Aristophanes are as ribald as the Sargus, and as virtuous in ritual and erudition as the Cantharus is in love. *Ulysses* resembles the trout, which is sick and lousy in the brook before the sun has warmed it.

Many passages cannot be quoted, because they nauseate the mind. Thoreau has said, "The imagination is wounded long before the conscience." What profit is there to go to the water-closet with Bloom? or, for that matter, to share the lechery of his wife Molly? When there is small erudition what else is there to write about save "warts, bunions and pimples," "the dirt that gets rolled up in your navel." The modern scatologist should heed the Ion of Euripides who takes his bow and aims it at the swan for dropping its ordure upon the statues.

Far from being what Wyndham Lewis calls a massive still-life, *Ulysses* is a Gargantuan urinal, without the laughter of Rabelais, or that author's plenteous reading of Pliny, Theophrastus, Cicero, Aristotle, Plato, and Antisthenes. We have the same W. C. rites in Kafka. Borrowing his title, *Metamorphosis*, from Ovid, and emptying that remarkable poet of myth and gods, he gives us a protagonist who has been translated into a cockroach. Take from man the Old Testament, the Greek thinkers, the Gospels, and the fables of the races, what else is he but a cockroach! Even if the heart is lotus-eaten, and we are morally numb, would not natural sense tell us this is wrong? As La Bruyère says, in all societies common sense gives way first.

The scatophagous *Metamorphosis* is opposite to the Homeric epic; Kafka, too feeble for heroic elemental nature, reduces man to a putrid insect that can hardly turn over on its back, whereas the smallest stones hurled by Ajax or Hector are boulders quarried by gigantic hands.

James Joyce cannot make the epic he obviously intended; Alfieri grieved and raved because the government gave no homage to ancient Roman heroes. Joyce's inability to create a colossus, despite the Homeric title of the novel, and the eponymous name of the protagonist, Dedalus, accounts for the froward language. The humor is an avoidance of the tragedy inherent in the book; wit cannot stand long against truth, declared Dr. Johnson.

The book genders sundry confusions, because there are no symbolical characters, a Thersites to represent foul words, Ajax stupidity, and Nestor the wisdom of experience. Joyce, to borrow from Richard Savage, is a Hackney Iscariot. The novel is without the light in which the angels are apparelled; Dedalus is a noctambulist, and the entire narrative is clothed in night. The Thracians used white stones as marks for their propitious days, and black for the unfortunate ones.

## *on* JAMES JOYCE: 5

DEAR HERBERT:

I must again return to this counterfeit titan, *Ulysses,* as it is the symptom of all our disgraces. Clement of Alexandria writes: "There is a difference between health and knowledge; for the latter is produced by learning and the former by healing"; and Ruskin says that words should comfort and not excite.

What is not foul and the evil droppings of our dreams in *Ulysses* could be placed between the covers of a chapbook. Joyce fleers upon his own intellect and soul; whenever he was thoughtful he entered the swine of Gadarene. He was marred by a decorticating mockery which sapped all love or feeling. This species of unnatural irony, as you say, Herbert, in your essay on Swift, is the mark of an insincere age. To perceive is to be sincere. That fashionable irony was more flagrant in Joyce than in Swift, and again I go to you on Swift, and made him so corrupt that he "could not say that good is *simply* good." Vauvenargues, with whom you have much greater familiarity than I, reminds us that mediocre minds do not feel the extremes of good and evil. Joyce's farthest limit

was remorse of conscience, not repentance. He repeats
Agenbite of Inwit, as though it were a medieval amulet
that might relieve him of the pains of turpitude.

*Ulysses* is the funerary orgy of Priapus; Phallus is
dead; long live the aproned Hercules, adept with the
distaff. Joyce says Sokrates was henpecked, Aristotle
bridled by an hetaera, and Shakespeare shrew-ridden.

Venus Vulgivaga Popularis, the bitch of pleasure,
dominates every page. Where is the chaste vision without which we are stupid weeds all our days, or any absolute, as Seven in the Kabala, or the Pythagorean tetrad,
which has angelical properties? The novel is altogether
reechy, and, despite the allusions to parturition, it is not
Diana, the obstetrical goddess, who attends the woman
in her throes, but a gamp, a bawdy nurse for pregnant
whores and blowsy minxes.

Joyce spawned a water-closet Eros who furnishes
Bloom with disgusting, flagellating words to awaken his
secret parts. Youth in Attica carried pieces of amatory
Mandrakes in their satchels; but Bloom's aphrodisiacs
are the garter and petticoat of a Dublin chit. When the
linen of Sheba, or Liza of Tudor do not raise man's
blood, he has criminal visions of the spermal ejaculation
of a man just hanged. There is the same perverse worship of the male sperm in *Moby Dick, The Seven Pillars
of Wisdom,* and "The Man Who Died."

Joyce maintains William Shakespeare and Leopold
Bloom wear antlers, and both are horned, not by Taurus,

but one by Ann Hathaway, the other by Molly. The primal fathers in the Mesopotamian Valley have died in the loins of their dispersed children, who have been parted from that Cornucopia which, D. H. Lawrence said, Michelangelo filled with phallical acorns.

Shakespeare lost his manhood when Ann Hathaway filched his virginity in the rye field. The boy who was taken can never be the man who takes. In *Othello*, says Joyce, Shakespeare is bawd and cuckold; the Blacka-moor is Iago deflowered of the hunter's blood; Iago can riot or fox in any placket. Othello, the intellect's rood, is Shakespeare's horns.

The shrews and grimalkins of Tartarus rule the nup-tial couch, seducing the green springal, and only sub-mitting to some "unaccountable muskin" or "Darby Dullman." The consequence of this "tyrannous inconti-nence" is a "cropeared creature, or a crookback." We recognize the spawn of "blind rut" by "Harelip, breast-mole, supernumerary digits, negro's inkle." The male is deformed, the clubfooted Byron, the valetudinary Pope, the crookback Richard who woos Ann (Ann Hathaway as Joyce avers), and Kierkegaard who looked upon his own hump as a carnal bequest from Richard the III; Kierkegaard at twenty-five thought he was too old for procreation.

The interpretation of Hamlet is wanton, for Joyce be-longed to that school of letters in which the perverse is the Angel of genius. Lust wastes truth, and wit, un-

gyvved, whores; every book is Hamlet's ghost, or our
rank weeds rotting on Lethe Wharf. I do not deny that
Shakespeare had the riggish intellect to create *Measure
for Measure*, but that the grape had raveled.

Hamlet has no progenitor, according to Joyce, since
his father is his own bitterness. Shakespeare has no
paternal origin; "John Shakespeare" is "divested of
fatherhood." Boccaccio's Calandrino, writes Joyce, was
the first and last man "who felt himself with child." In
*Genesis* it is said that Adam and not Eve bare Seth. We
are told the names of Noah's three sons, but who was his
wife? The daughters of Lot seduced their father, for it is
the seed of the father that is coveted and which begins a
new race. Jacob gives the blessing and the birthright to
the tribes. Simeon and Levi are cruel swords, Benjamin
is a ravening wolf, and the fat loaves of Judea shall
come from Asher. This is patriarchic authority and perception of Jacob the Begetter.

The laws are from Abraham and Moses, and the genealogy of the races is, Abraham begat Isaac and Isaac
Jacob. Style, too, comes from the genitalia of the gods;
Isis, the ancient one, searches for the procreative organs
of Osiris.

The reign of Adam, Noah and Lot is at an end, and
the rule of the shrew over the boy Shakespeare begins.
When men are boys there is no father and son; the boy-
women of the Shakespearean comedies are the catamites
in the imagination of Joyce. Joyce writes, "I asked him
what he thought of the charge of pederasty brought

against the bard. He lifted his hands and said: All we can say is that life ran high in those days." The author cringes before the patriarch. "It is this fear," writes William Carlos Williams, "that drives us to the homosexual out of dread of our fathers." This is the reason for that ruined runic in the novel, Agenbite of Inwit, Inwit's Agenbite, which is the cry of the sea, the elements to save him from that nether sin. There is no right or wrong in *Ulysses*, only sexual sin, that remorse of conscience, which will give him no quiet. Agenbite plagues the veiny blood which cannot close its maw, but neighs and drinks up more darkness and scortatory pleasures, called by St. Thomas, the avarice of the emotions: incest, Ammon's desire for his sister Tamar, Pasiphae's union with a bull, and pederasty which Gide canonized in *If It Die*.

The Ghost declares that his lightest words would harrow up the soul of Hamlet, which no father could say to any son who was not the kin and marrow of his identity. The author of *Ulysses* claims: "Who is the father of any son that any son should love him or he any son." "What links them in nature? An instant of blind rut."

If Hamlet has no father, and the ghost is his own bile and moan, is Hamlet impotent? Is the fever for Ophelia the canting song of sere bones? Does Hamlet batten upon the griefs and the corse of the father? Are Hamlet's vows unto the ghost the oaths of a father-hater? Does he go mad, or feign to, to sup upon the specter? When the ghost flees as the cock crows, is it the horror and fear of the son which wastes his rueful substance? The son's growth "is his father's decline, his youth his father's envy."

The book is intractably lascivious; no cakes of salt or sesame are offered to the piacular deities who might dispel those unholy loves which have shaken the blood and the judgment of a whole age. He did not endeavor to mitigate those Stygian diseases of which incest, parricide, and sodomy are wrought. "Let set times be appointed, and certain hours be ordered for the health of our soul," said St. Augustine.

Joyce was Catholic, separated no less than Bloom, from the fathers of his faith, and he wrote like an unfrocked, libidinous priest who has no Petrine rock to sustain him. It is odd that the sodality of atheistical scribbling Nimrods, pining for the old debaucheries in the Plains of Shinar, should have turned to James Joyce whose book was gnawed to pieces by a shame of his own foul desires.

James Joyce forsook the great Christian fathers, who had been his sages, and he obviously abhorred any paternal legislation. For all the nonsense regarding his endeavor to revivify the Gaelic, his language is as incontinent as his spirit. The special genius of Ireland, wrote George Moore, is celibacy. I am not suggesting that an author be ascetic, but no book can be all Dead Sea lust, and not be a vile draught of night. "Perhaps," asserted Dr. Johnson, "neither Pope nor Boileau has made the world much better than he found it." James Joyce left it far worse.

He wrote as though once freed from the teachings of Jerome, Tertullian, and Origen, he could fill his imaginings that are like the holes in the bucket into which the daughters of Danaus incessantly pour water. One cannot exchange a Christian for a pagan thinker, and assume that Lucian or Martial give him leave to be the most putrid and gorbellied Caliban in the earth. *The Odes*, a breviary for any pensive Catholic, says that our sins forbid Jove to lay aside his thunderbolts.

Suppose that one were no better than a moth or an humuncio, is there nothing else but levity, dirt, and fornication? There is no wish on my part to dismiss Venus Mandragoritis, or to forget what nectar flows from her mouth and cestus, but are we no more than brutal matter itching, scraping and gendering for over seven hundred and fifty pages. Does a whole tome have to exhale the gases of a Chimaera, and is there not one gentle zephyr, as Kierkegaard has said, blowing from the groves of Mamre. "May Christ's dove come among us, or else Minerva's owl," says Erasmus. It is a common defect in those poisonous and epicene corybantes who personate Bacchic matrons crying out *Evoi* as they hold the phalloi aloft, to assert that every savant and poet was a pathic.

The sayings of the Gospels, which have been the honey in our wretched, terrene bodies, are garbled, and smell of the moth, corruption and the stews. What does Joyce prove in writing that Christ is himself his own Father and Son: "The consubstantiality of the Son with the Father." His speculation is not only as vain as the medieval disputation about baptism or synaxis, but has a malefic motive. The Catholic grammar of Duns Scotus or Aquinas becomes the darkling syllogisms of Ham. The sole purpose is parricide, to cast into Limbo THOU SHALT NOT, which is the law of the Father. Thou Shalt Not lie, steal, cheat, commit sodomy, are abhorrent once good and evil are despised; and anyone who utters a truth has dropped an acorn which will produce his own wilderness.

## *on* JAMES JOYCE: 6

DEAR EDWARD:

What is my rôle in this exchange of letters? To be *advocatus diaboli*, and to find some few virtues, some extenuating circumstances, to throw into the scales you have so heavily weighted with your wrath? If I am to be honest I must admit most of the charges you bring against Joyce, and then my scant pleadings will seem so sentimental.—A black villain, Sir, but he hath a pretty child; and once I saw him give a crust to a beggar . . .

I said in my last letter that Joyce had been a revelation to me when I first began to read him. It was not *Ulysses*, however, that seduced me, but *A Portrait of the Artist as a Young Man*. This book was published in 1916, in the middle of the War, and the reading of Joyce, as of Henry James and D. H. Lawrence, was part of my war experience—they were my rations on the march, in trenches and billets, and their world of art kept me sane in an atmosphere of blood and death. I mention this fact only to excuse what was no doubt an emotional approach—and the emotion lingers. I was reading these authors with the consciousness that they represented creative possibilities that might at any moment be for ever snatched from me. Dr. Johnson said that the thought of death by hanging had a wonderfully sobering effect on a man: and I would say that there is nothing like the constant danger of death for sharpening a man's sensibilities. I read these authors with that advantage.

You continue, in a welcome spate of letters, to concentrate on *Ulysses,* and rightly so because it is Joyce's most famous book. I doubt if it contains his best writing, which may be in *Dubliners.* But I have lost my copy of that volume of stories, and have no grateful memories of it. The *Portrait,* however, is another question. I still have my copy of the first edition, and its state bears witness to the frequent use I made of it when I was twenty-three! I turn again to its foxed pages and try to recover its vanished magic. (Joyce, by the way, gave it a motto from Ovid that should appeal to you: *Et ignotas animum dimittit in artes.*) Oh, yes: it is there—all the forgotten anguish of adolescence, the fierce longings of the bruised heart, the lyrical evocations of unsatisfied lust. Listen to this:

> A girl stood before him in midstream: alone and still, gazing out to sea. She seemed like one whom magic had changed into the likeness of a strange and beautiful seabird. Her long slender bare legs were delicate as a crane's and pure save where an emerald trail of seaweed had fashioned itself as a sign upon the flesh. Her thighs,

fuller and softhued as ivory, were bared almost
to the hips where the white fringes of her drawers
were like feathering of soft white down. Her
slate-blue skirts were kilted boldly about her
waist and dove-tailed behind her. Her bosom was
as a bird's, soft and slight, slight and soft as the
breast of some dark-plumaged dove. But her
long fair hair was girlish: and girlish, and
touched with the wonder of mortal beauty, her
face.

She was alone and still, gazing out to sea; and
when she felt his presence and the worship of his
eyes her eyes turned to him in quiet sufferance of
his gaze, without shame or wantonness. Long,
long she suffered his gaze and then quietly with-
drew her eyes from his and bent them towards
the stream, gently stirring the water with her foot
hither and thither. The first faint noise of gently
moving water broke the silence, low and faint
and whispering, faint as the bells of sleep; hither
and thither, hither thither: and a faint flame
trembled on her cheek.

Did your patience last to the end? It is Pater and milk,
sweet and sentimental—I know it all and I am not going
to defend it as mature art (though I can see its connection with the later style, even with the hitherings and
thitherings of the Liffey in *Finnegans Wake*). I am only
trying to explain why Joyce had such a strong appeal to
me in the year 1916. I was seduced by the music in these

sentences, by their carefully modulated rhythm, their colour and vision (that "trail of seaweed"—all unconsciously I put it into a poem years later!).

But all this sweetness, all this artful delicacy, was to be destroyed, deliberately.

When Joyce left Dublin, left the provincial atmosphere of Ireland and became a European, he quickly recognized himself for what he was: a sentimentalist and a romanticist; and all his subsequent work was an attempt to disguise this defect. No doubt there is ironic detachment in his early work; but that also can be a romantic pose. The way Joyce attempted to disguise his real nature was first to pretend to a classical form (the structural parallelism with Homer's work), and then, since this did not suffice, to break down the rhythms of his prose style (for the style being the man himself, it is the style that must be the mask).

I return to my personal experiences with *Ulysses*. When I received my copy of the first edition from Paris (I had ordered it before publication, so it reached me before the censor had had a chance to put his foul hands on it), I found myself in possession of a volume the size of a telephone directory, bound in flimsy blue paper. I took it to an old bookbinder in London, and he showed me a piece of ancient vellum, which I eagerly selected. *Ulysses* became an ivory incunabulum, and I read it with the piety that a hermit would devote to his breviary.

Six years ran between the publication of *A Portrait* and *Ulysses*, though they had been by the stepping-stones of the excerpts published in *The Egoist* and *The Little Review*. Nevertheless, the difference between the two books was enough to constitute a shock. There was a certain continuity of style:

> Woodshadows floated silently by through the morning peace from the stairhead seaward where he gazed. Inshore and farther out the mirror of water whitened, spurned by lightshod hurrying feet. White breast of the dim sea. The twining stresses, two by two. A hand plucking the harpstrings merging their twining cords. Wavewhite wedded words shimmering on the dim tide.

This is comparable to the passage I have quoted from *A Portrait,* though the sentences are now shorter, the rhythm now staccato. But in 1922 it was still exciting to me, and when it passed from a lyrical to a realistic content, I could admire it all the more: I too had become cynically mature. Now read the scene in the Burton restaurant—I cannot quote the whole of it (it begins on page 161 in the first edition). I am not concerned for the moment with the question of realism—read it for its style, and let us take these sentences as a specimen:

> Perched on high stools by the bar, hats shoved back, at the tables calling for more bread no charge, swilling, wolfing gobfuls of sloppy food, their eyes bulging, wiping wetted moustaches. A pallid suetfaced young man polished his tumbler

knife fork and spoon with his napkin. New set
of microbes. A man with an infant's saucestained
napkin tucked round him shovelled gurgling
soup down his gullet: no teeth to chewchewchew
it. Chump chop from the grill. Bolting to get it
over. Sad booser's eyes. Bitten off more than he
can chew. Am I like that? See ourselves as others
see us. Hungry man is an angry man. Working
tooth and jaw. Don't! O! A bone! That last
pagan king of Ireland Cormac in the schoolpoem
choked himself at Sletty southward of the Boyne.
Wonder what he was eating. Something galop-
tious. Saint Patrick converted him to Christian-
ity. Couldn't swallow it all however.
  —Roast beef and cabbage.
  —One stew.
Smells of men. His gorge rose. Spaton sawdust, sweetish warmish cigarette smoke, reek of
plug, spilt beer, men's beery piss, the stale of
ferment.

Asthmatic shortness of breath? You might as well say
that the bristles in Breughel's paintbrush were too short.
Syntactic criticism is irrelevant if words are doing their
work. And for page after page Joyce's words are doing
good work, communicating his impressionistic vision of
the world of reality.

But already in *Ulysses* there are many signs of that
"metaphysical nihilism" (the phrase was used by Ernst
Robert Curtius in one of the best essays ever written on

Joyce) which led to a complete disruption of grammar
and syntax, to a failure in communication.

We need not indulge in a pedantic criticism of the interior monologue. Personally I believe that as an experiment, a *tour de force*, Molly Bloom's dialogue at the end
of *Ulysses* justifies itself. It is the sheer act of intuition
that amazes me—for a man to *be* a Dublin trollop for
25,000 consecutive words, with never an intrusion of
the masculine, of the objective, of the judgmental. The
stream of that consciousness was muddy, you will say,
a section of a city sewer rather than the motions of a
mind that we can contemplate as *human*. But another
Irishman before Joyce gave us a picture of a city sewer,
and even of the contents of a woman's mind ("Mrs. Har-
ris's Petition"). Swift had no finer feelings on the subject, and you admire Swift.

*Ulysses* is a novel of darkness, as you say, but it is just
that that makes it a novel of our time. We live in an
eternal spiritual darkness, and to bear witness to the
fact, as Joyce does, is not to betray the functions of the
artist. I am with you in preferring an author who lifts
up a lantern of idealism amid that darkness, however
dim and guttering. I shall insist that both Henry James
and D. H. Lawrence did this. But Joyce had lost his
faith, in man and in God, and was without any hope of
human betterment. But must we make of this a *literary*
judgment? Had Swift more hope? No, you will say, but
he had a sense of good and evil. And so, I believe, had
Joyce. But a *sense*, not censoriousness!

Jaspers says (in a book called *Reason and Existenz*) that Kierkegaard "had a certain police talent, to be spy in the service of the divinity. He uncovered, but he did not assert what should be done." That would serve as a description of Joyce, too, though I do not suggest that there is anything in common between Joyce and Kierkegaard, except that they were both born in a bog. That there should be "no right or wrong" in *Ulysses* I hold to be artistically right; and if there is *even* "sexual sin, that remorse of conscience," I should not think Joyce the less a true poet. But remorse there may be, and, as I have argued in my *Wordsworth*, remorse is the most destructive force that can enter an artist's consciousness. In Dublin they blame Joyce for deserting his family. Joyce's remorse may be as simple as that, and have nothing to do, directly, with sex. But it hurts his whole output: it is at the root of what I feel to be your strongest charge against him—that he could not be contemplative because he thought it more important to be humorous. Humorous? That is too healthy a word. Punning, word-spawning, all the dreary riddles of *Finnegans Wake*— that is not humour, not even *humeur noire*. It is the desperate obliquity of a man who can no longer look reality in the face.

So I end by joining you in condemning Joyce—or rather, in acquiescing in Joyce's own self-condemnation, Finnegan's suicide, the polyglot bog to which the Irish genius returned, in which he sank.

There are no perfect books in this age of ours—we

need not look for them, for they cannot be created out of our intellectual self-consciousness—Lawrence was the last to try. But among the many half-lights, the broken images of a brighter day, are some few pages that Joyce wrote. Acknowledge them, and pass on.

on D. H. LAWRENCE

## *on* D. H. LAWRENCE: 1

DEAR EDWARD:

I must excuse myself for writing so dispropor-
tionately little about Joyce, but I am anxious to pass on
to two writers whom I consider much more ambiguous
and therefore much more in need of our questioning
scrutiny—D. H. Lawrence and Henry James. The easiest
transition is to Lawrence. I doubt if James ever became
aware of the existence of Joyce—I know of no recorded
judgment, but his attitude of disdain towards Dostoevsky
would naturally have been extended to the author of
*Ulysses*. He called Dostoevsky's novels "fluid pud-
dings"; which is much the same phrase that Lawrence
used about Joyce's work. "My God! What a clumsy *olla
putrida* James Joyce is!" he writes in one of his letters
(to Maria and Aldous Huxley, 15 August, 1928). "Nothing but old fags and cabbage stumps of quotations from
the Bible and the rest, stewed in the juice of deliberate, journalistic dirty-mindedness—what old and hard-
worked staleness, masquerading as the all-new!" This is
no doubt the Band of Hope Lawrence, the Lawrence that
remained a prude even when writing *Lady Chatterley's*

*Lover* (which might be called *The Prude's Revenge*—
revenge for those early years of pious repression). But
Lawrence had an aesthetic basis, too, for his reaction—
he found Joyce's method, his writing, "too terribly
would-be and done-on-purpose, utterly without spon-
taneity or real life." An aesthetic judgment of some kind
lurks in such phrases, and it is one that we shall have
to extend to Lawrence's own work. However, let me, before I have done with Joyce, say this in defense of his
*olla putrida:* if one takes a lucky dip into it, one will
often find a delicious morsel in the spoon. His writing
reminds me of that now so fashionable mode of painting associated with the name of Jackson Pollock. It looks
like the dribbles and splashes made on a kitchen floor by
a cook with Parkinson's disease, and is actually produced by a similar process. The over-all effect is of no
more interest than such a kitchen floor, but isolate a
small patch no bigger than a hand and you have as often
as not a design as exquisite as a fragment of a Coptic
textile, or a shard of Persian faience. I don't *see* the
painting as a whole, nor the novel as a whole, and I don't
believe a wholeness exists, in spite of Joyce's own pre-
tensions and the claims of his exegetes. But these fragments, which we accidentally unpiece from the chaos—
they are bright and potent.

A modest achievement, and that is why I would not
devote more space to it. As for the putrid element, which
is the real basis of Lawrence's violent reaction (and
even of yours?)—let us take it in the clinical spirit of

our criticism. It is a monster that Lawrence himself struggled with, and the spectacle is of some interest.

I shall maintain that Lawrence, all things considered, is the greatest "writer" of our generation; but great, not as an artist, but as a moralist. He is a moralist of a pattern that is ancient enough to seem very new to us—a prophet of the Hebraic stature, fierce, passionate, and even inspired. As an artist, however, he is not merely flawed: he is grotesque.

He knew he was a moralist, and this drove him to assert (in his great dithyrambic sermon on Whitman) that the essential function of art *is* moral. "Not aesthetic, not decorative, not pastime and recreation. But moral. The essential function of art is moral."

And then, as if slightly uneasy to have uttered such a brash challenge, he adds:

"But a passionate, implicit morality, not didactic. A morality which changes the blood, rather than the mind. Changes the blood first. The mind follows later, in the wake."

What a blessed word *implicit* is! Some residue of aesthetic sensibility told Lawrence that the morality *ought* to be implicit in art (as it is implicit in Henry James's art); but in his own work it is always blatantly explicit. And it is that that makes him a prophet rather than an artist.

The novels are relentlessly crude, in plot, in characterization, in form and style and atmosphere—in everything that can justify the novel as a work of art. Had his

novels not been vehicles for a very explicit morality—
a new and a very necessary morality—they would never
have been given serious consideration. (There is another
reason, but to discuss it might be embarrassing to some
worthy people: I mean that his novels exude some *res-
sentiment* of the little man, perhaps of the provincial
little man, of the little man who imagines that he is
despised by women; so that people of this kind, who
sense this strain in Lawrence, become his passionate
advocates.) His novels have, of course, their patches of
beauty—not accidental fragments, as in *Ulysses*, but
deliberate patches, exercises in lyricism. They are frequent in early works like *The White Peacock*, dwindling
as time went on, and almost totally absent from the
tough-guy crudity of *Lady Chatterley's Lover* (where in
fiction is a figure of such grotesque crudity as Mellors,
the erotic gamekeeper, Pan in corduroy breeches, a goat
with a shotgun?) But these are the extremes: the best of
Lawrence's work comes in his middle period, and we are
asked to judge him by *The Rainbow* and *Women in
Love*. Dr. Leavis, in his recent book on Lawrence, claims
that these are the greatest novels in the English language; and Angus Wilson, reviewing Dr. Leavis's book
in a recent issue of *Encounter*, says that *Women in
Love* "has a form as strict as some court dance." A *court*
dance! Perhaps a folk dance, to the music of scrannel
pipes—one cannot deny that there is some impulsive
energy at play!

When these critics further dilate on the "characterization" in Lawrence's novels (and we are all agreed that characterization is the specific function of the novel—in structure it can have much in common with the drama), they take advantage of the ambiguity of the term. Lawrence was incapable of *inventing* a character, in the sense that Tom Jones is a character, or Emma Bovary, or Milly Theale. He had no gift for imaginative *creation*. The people in his novels are either projections of himself, as is Birkin in *Women in Love,* or they are descriptions (caricatures, rather) of people he knew in real life. The novel (if it is a work of art) is no more a transcript of real life, a portraiture of actual characters, than a painting (if it too is a work of art) is the transcript of the visible scene. (We have a word for such transcripts—journalism, or *reportage.*) There is no art anywhere unless the human experience has passed through the alembic of the imagination, and we are given, not a replica of sensational or intellectual data, but a transfiguration of these raw materials. Art is creation, an extension of experience, of consciousness itself; it is not—Edward, you must agree—it is *not* "a complete moral truth that is a final criticism of modern Western society!"

I have no wish to criticize Lawrence for faults that are endemic to the modern novel as such—its fatal lack of style or form, its universal banality and triviality of observation. "He rose, and came to the door, wiping his mouth with a red handkerchief, still chewing." That is the kind of sentence you will find in any average novel of today. Sixteen words: write five thousand such sentences and you have a novel! But why should you or I or any sober man be interested in such a banal statement of fact? "The sun shone into the bare room, which still smelled of a mutton chop, done in a dutch oven before the fire, because the dutch oven still stood on the fender, with the black potato-saucepan on a piece of paper, beside it on the white hearth. The fire was red, rather low, the bar dropped, the kettle singing." And so it goes on, page after page, incredibly credible—"On the table was his plate, with potatoes and the remains of the chop; also bread in a basket, salt, and a blue mug with beer. The tablecloth was white oilcloth. He stood in the shade."

Such is Lawrence's prose style, and we are expected to read it, not once as we read a newspaper report, but repeatedly, for this is supposedly an art: classical, traditional, universal! Reserve those words, it will be said, for the art of the past: this is realism, as eternal as a mutton chop or a mug on a table, as eternal as the pair of boots or the kitchen chair that Van Gogh painted (I shall probably return to this comparison). But no! In a work of art every detail is present by virtue of its strict necessity—its bearing on character and atmosphere, its contribution to development and form. An apologist for Lawrence would no doubt be prepared to argue that all the banal details in this paragraph do contribute to the characterization of the erotic gamekeeper—that his handkerchief was essentially *red,* his saucepan *black,* his mug *blue;* that at this particular moment in the development of the plot, he should be wiping his mouth, chewing, standing in the shade. Well, if so, I can only say that for me he is a boring character, completely without subtlety or nuance, vulgar in kind and conception.

But, the apologists will say, Lawrence adopted the only means in his power to propagate his message. People will read novels, five thousand, even fifty thousand banal sentences. They will not nowadays listen to sermons, or read essays, however short and pithy. I sympathize with Lawrence in his dilemma, and I would not criticize him for so cynically abusing an art form did not his apologists see no cynicism in it. They go further than this—they tend to blame Lawrence for his naïveté —the "genius, but . . ." attitude of our friend Aldington. If only Lawrence had not read Whitman and Freud, if only he hadn't had such a passion for reforming the world, what a fine artist he would have been! I believe this to be a faithless and treacherous attitude to Lawrence. Lawrence was what he was, not because he had read Whitman and Freud, but because he was the son of Arthur Lawrence, a miner, and Lydia Lawrence, a school-teacher; because he was born in a mining village and brought up with two brothers and two sisters, because of all the specific genetic and environmental reasons that went to his make-up. He could not have been otherwise than he was, as a personality, and the only question is whether he chose the right means of expressing that personality and its acquired characteristics.

He might have become a painter, for example. One of

the deprivations forced on us by our inhuman civilization is that we are no longer trained to express ourselves
sensuously, in the materials of craft. Lawrence had a
direct response to color and form: he saw the vivid natural details and could describe them. The same twelfth
chapter of *Lady Chatterley's Lover* from which I have
been quoting opens with a description of a wood in late
Spring:

> Yellow celandines now were in crowds, flat open,
> pressed back in urgency, and the yellow glitter
> of themselves. It was the yellow, the powerful
> yellow of early summer. And primroses were
> broad, and full of pale abandon, thick-clustered
> primroses no longer shy. The lush, dark green of
> hyacinths was a sea, with buds rising like pale
> corn, while in the riding the forget-me-nots were
> fluffing up, and columbines were unfolding their
> ink-purple ruches, and there were bits of blue
> bird's-egg-shell under a bush.

It has its syntactical crudities, it is the writing of an
immature schoolboy, and it reeks of the pathetic fallacy,
but there is also intensity of vision—no mutton chops
and mugs of beer, which remain mutton chops and mugs
of beer however long you observe them; but yellow that
is *powerful* just at that moment of vision, in early summer; and primroses that are *broad,* no longer shy; and
the buds of hyacinths like *pale corn;* and the forget-me-
nots *fluffing up;* and the bits of blue egg-shell which bring

the whole scene into instantaneous focus. How lame are such words as "shy" and "pale" and "bits," but in spite of them a sensation is conveyed.

I once quoted a long passage from *The White Peacock* as an admirable example of "emotive prose." I have just read it again. Yes: it has paragraphs as good (but no better) than this description of a wood—again acute observation of birds and again it is the moment when "my whole world thrilled with the conception of summer." It is a description of a funeral procession through the countryside. What I still find excellent, however, are not the rather routine evocations of birds and flowers: these I now find sentimental ("There the daffodils were lifting their heads and throwing back their yellow curls"—the whole passage is full of such false pathos). More acute are observations that must have been based on a more unusual experience—the coffin of "new unpolished wood, gleaming and glistening in the sunlight; the men who carry it will remember all their lives the smell of new, warm elm-wood." That I still find evocative—or is it nostalgic?

In this respect Lawrence cannot compete with Joyce: Joyce has the same rawness of sensibility, and the ability to dispense with the salve of sentiment. Joyce's style, as I have argued elsewhere (*A Coat of Many Colours*) is a mask for sentiment, even for sentimentality. But the mask is often beautifully carved.

You objected, in your last letter, to Lawrence's obsessional use of a limited range of epithets, and we might well judge our authors by the adjectives they use. The best writers avoid the bruised outlines adjectives are apt to give to a sentence, and above all they eschew the adjectival participle, or whatever the grammarians call it —the word that drags a tail of ugly sound behind it, just as they eschew sentimental diminutives—little, tiny, etc. You say that Lawrence's neologisms leave us mad: I prefer them to his sick, sweet use of old words.

A weak style ill becomes a moralist—can one imagine Swift or Vauvenargues, Spinoza or Kierkegaard, writing in the stuttering, repetitive manner of Lawrence? I am with you in equating an author's style and his morals— twenty years ago I wrote "Prose is as various as mankind itself; it only ceases to be of interest when it expresses, not the man himself, but a convention, or a confusion, or an unresolved impression. There is something immoral about bad prose." Lawrence dispenses with grace in the desire to be "immediate," "instantaneous," "pulsating"—to be, that is to say, a particular kind of moralist. But if the essential function of art is to be moral, it must still be art! Morality relieved by lyrical outcries is not a recipe for novel-writing, and if you protest, as our old friend Ford used to protest, that the novel is a glorious rag-bag that can accommodate anything, absolutely anything, then I merely stubbornly assert that a rag-bag is not a work of art; and that what we are trying to do in this exchange of letters is to isolate from the *olla putrida*, the literary mish-mash fed to us daily, the few genuine works of art.

I doubt if Lawrence wrote a book that will survive as a single, separate, wholesome work of art. The short stories are no better than the novels; even the much-praised "St. Mawr"—which is neither a novel nor a short-story—is but a halting parable, an awkwardly told allegory. A fantasy like "The Man Who Died" is more shapely; but even this work is another tract, and loathsome in its implications. It is again the work of a moralist, not of an artist. But to this distinction I will return in my next letter.

## *on* D. H. LAWRENCE: 2

DEAR HERBERT:

Nostalgia, my dear Herbert, is a stumbling-block to perception. You are homesick for your memories, which is no better than the Lotophagi who forgets them. Who can recollect the remote and vapory impressions of his youth?

I like very much your allusion to Dr. Johnson on death which sharpened your own spirit as you read. Should we not always read as though we were dying?

However, Herbert, when you take one thing that is short, such as the very shabby sentences of Joyce in *Ulysses,* and compare them with the short bristles of Breughel, I think you err. Two things that are short are not necessarily equal to one another, any more than if I have one arm much longer than the other am I Artaxerxes.

I write you with a heavy, torpid heart. We have seen so many of our confraternity fall into the dust, their bones still fresh labor for the maggots. We had a plethora of affection for them, and we believed that their works were the massive Inca stones of broken huacas and the fanes of Quito. Alas, poor ghosts!

For myself, D. H. Lawrence, Ford Madox Ford, Theodore Dreiser, Sherwood Anderson, still breathe in me as the Ephesian sod. It is a double hardship to cast their poems, novels and tracts into Tartarus. How kind they were; aged, asthmatic Ford fatly shuffling down Eighth Street, and begging you to come to see him, or to bring him the last book you had published. He had windmills in his brain, and had such a prodigal heart that he invited people to come to his southern manor which never existed.

Baudelaire, Stendhal, and Flaubert hated Paris, and is there a place where solitude is such a brutal epicure's pleasure as in Montmartre. In Paris I had one of those seizures of bitter, claustral loneliness which attack the exile whose salon is in the street. I went out to Seine-Suresne where Lawrence was staying with some other people. At the door I heard the noise and the cymbals of flesh inside, and when Lawrence came to the door I hungered to be among the pagans of letters. When he said he could not ask me in, my face plainly spoke, "your books are the hot gods of Attica; touch me, or I stink like Lazarus." That nimble, russet satyr asked me to see him the next day at the Café des Deux Magots.

Now, most of his work is chaff in my mouth. He wrote far too much, always changing the stones into bread. Every century has its own derisive cherub, and ours is the terrible Angel of Waste. Coleridge wrote, ". . . I would address an affectionate exhortation to the youthful literati, grounded on my own experience. It will be but short; for the beginning, middle, and end converge to one charge: NEVER PURSUE LITERATURE AS A TRADE." Herder made this observation: "A person, who reads only to print, in all probability reads amiss; and he, who sends away through the pen and the press every thought, the moment it occurs to him, will in a short time have sent all away, and will become a mere journeyman of the printing office, a compositor." Edmund Spenser brings Guion through the cave of Mammon, showing him that bower of earthly bliss, and from which he abstains. Lawrence could have been such a palmer! What guerdon might have been his, and ours, in return for a vow of poverty. Herbert, well, might your late friend, Eric Gill, write, God bless indigence.

In a way, we are, as Milton has it in the *Areopagitica*, *muselesse and unboekish*. Very little has been written by those who promised us much. Are we exhausted? Our woe goes back farther than Lawrence, Kierkegaard, or Flaubert. Every one of these men suffered from a kind of senility. Kierkegaard was an ennuyed Mephisto who said that "the highest thing a woman can do for a man is to come within his range at the right instant, and that the greatest thing she can do after that is to be unfaithful to him." Flaubert at thirty-six was already devoured by boredom; Rimbaud wrote, "I die of lassitude. It is the tomb. . . ."

English and American, we are not the heirs of Spenser, Gower, Surrey, Keats, Coleridge, but of Flaubert, Stendhal, Balzac, Rimbaud, Baudelaire, those hierophantic rakes of hell. No wonder then that we have had a half century of tired volumes. The seven lean kine have devoured the seven fat ones, and there has been no Joseph to stuff Pharaoh's granaries against the time of famine.

Herbert, I was always weary, and long before I had ever heard of Baudelaire or Verlaine, I knew the grandeur of the pariah, Baudelaire's phrase. I have been in exile since my earliest years, and no banished man has much strength. My soul was aged at six, and torpor, which is the result of living apart from men, was mine. Mr. Isherwood, in his preface to Baudelaire's *Intimate Journals*, has said, "Baudelaire suffered constantly from Acedia, 'the malady of Monks,' that deadly weakness of the will which is the root of all evil." That explains surrealism, which is the reliance upon the dream after the guttering of volition. We are all surrealists, or existentialists, because the will died when the pylons and sphinxes crumbled in the Thebaid.

There is much contempt for learning in our age. The illiterate fishermen of Galilee understood homely adages which are either unknown or inscrutable to the university professor. It is as froward of an author to be ignorant as it was for the Phaeacians to be without boats and oars. Hugh of St. Victor wrote: "For not to know something is far different from not wanting to know something, since not to know is a weakness, but to detest knowledge is a perversion of the will."

The season of the journeyman is at an end. Virgil went to Theophrastus for the horticulture in the *Bucolics* and *Georgics;* Elisha first poured water on the hands of the prophet Elijah to apprentice himself to the work of truth. A master begets a poet or a sage as Abraham begat Isaac and Isaac bare Jacob. Milton retired into solitude for five years to read the ancients before he began *Paradise Lost.* Dostoevsky's work was healed by the Epistles of St. Paul; but Lawrence had no Homer, Catullus or Izaak Walton to guide him.

Our poor moiety of learning comes from an Atlean belief in the times; La Fontaine questioned the sanity of any one who preferred his own age to antiquity. There was never such tumid scorn of the past, and at the very root of this mean, crusty arrogance is the lack of awe, the reverence for human wisdom which one Chinese showed by inscribing a wise saying on the bone of Buddha. I remember your own plaint, Herbert, in "Mutations of the Phoenix."

> Beauty, truth and rarity,
> Grace in all simplicity,
> Here enclosed in cinders lie.

Lawrence wanted above all to be a barbarian of Eden; he desired to write like a primordial child, and so he adopted the humbug, primitive innocence of Gertrude Stein, who is the Hecate of his prose.

He was the raw, new genius; Chaucer and Gower were seeded by other poets, but Lawrence imagined his own afflatus to be like one of the mares in Lusitania who was said to have been impregnated by the winds. Ordinary sows, horses, she-goats need five to ten months for their gestation, but Lawrence suffered from an uninterrupted literary pregnancy. There was no fallow period between books to sow vetch, spelt, lupines or one apothegm. Each animal has its own rut-time; sheep conceive best at the setting of Arcturus, but Lawrence thought he was in-tuitive all the year round. A more reflective aboriginal would have considered the heifer and the lilies; we may learn from the laurel or the ash when we may bear fruit or know when we are barren.

One goes to literature for the deciduous tree as well as the evergreen; the olive and the vine growing in the mountains are barren, and that is good too; not all the fruits of Minerva are for eating.

Lawrence dotes on a stale chit of a word as though it were Catullus's minion; what affection for the English of Chaucer, Skelton and Milton is there in an author whose sole adjectival refrain is "dark," "wild," "bright," "quick," "repulsive," "repellent," "germinating," "puls-ing." His sentences lack the strength of stones, crags, ravines, or bracken; the honey is in the lion's carcase, or as Hesiod asserts, the holm-oak produces the bees. Lawrence depended upon intuitions which are likely to be a Judas or a Peter; the blood is as often fast asleep during the vigil as the twelve disciples.

Here are a few of the insipid puerilities, the "dark matrix," "dark hate," "dark lashes," which Lawrence thought were the mindless lambs of the Lord. *Mornings in Mexico* is the Adamic laugh of the diaphragm; the "long jowled . . . demonish parrots" and the dog, Corasmin, are the reasons for the primeval, abdominal mirth: "They make my diaphragm convulse with little laughs, almost mechanically," "One's diaphragm chuckles involuntarily," "It is a sound that penetrates one straight at the diaphragm," "curly little white Corasmin," "the toddling little curly white Corasmin," "like a little curly dog," "Corasmin is a little fat, curly white dog," "the little white curly Corasmin." Words poorly used leave us as restless as Lucifer going to and fro in the earth. Dullness, as you know, Herbert, is the pest of the muses: "black and bright and wild in the dark faces," "the hot, dark, intestinal blood," "the mysterious rhythm on the creative pulse," "the everlasting darkness, and the strange lifting and dropping, surging," "the circulating blood-stream dancing in the peril of his own isolation."

It was this "reptillian" hatred of the paleface which induced several thousand Anglo-American Amazons from Thermidon to abandon their husbands and to seek the marriage-bed of a Portuguese fisherman, a Negro, a waiter from Fiesole, a mestizo out of a Tasco cantino, or a drayman in Luzon.

English is dead, as Wyndham Lewis has observed; the language is no longer spoken in the universities or in the streets. The carter, the smith, the wright have gone to their graves. The peddlers of knives, pins, girdles, the hucksters of herbs, melons, thyme, and garlic have disappeared. It is good to know that the mother of Euripides was a vendor of herbs, to hear the humble chant of Amos: "I was a neatherd, and a gatherer of the Sycamore Fruits."

The usurer has killed the old bricks, the meadows, the heifer and the mares, and yet the rich have not on their tables the *wastel* bread fed to the best horses in medieval times. The demise of the handicrafts, followed by the cult of the NEW in letters, has given us sluttish words. The dialect of the artisans of Chaucer's age is not to be compared with the dead factory jargon of the auto grub. I found this remark of Ruskin in a Tolstoy letter: "It is physically impossible that true religious knowledge, or pure morality, should exist among any classes of a nation who do not work with their hands for their bread." I quote it, Herbert, because it is so close to your own feeling when you wrote of the city-hurt mind of a Hamlet "musing in the gutters."

Galilean parables come out of the mouths of fishers and vine-dressers; Jesus made ploughs and oxgoads, and the prophet Amos was also an angler. But where are the cummin seed, the anise, the "haws, hips, hazel nuts and acorns"; they are as far from us as the tales of a gryphon. When flour is well milled and the wagon sturdily wrought, the language of the people is plain and strong. As you say yourself in writing about George Herbert: "The simplicity of his style is due, first to an economy of imagery, and then to a conversational ease of diction."

We are mewed up like hawks, which makes us testy;

but there are many easing diets of prose for the unquiet. Izaak Walton remained halcyon through the commotions of King Charles and Cromwell. Alas, Walton, or Marvell, or Dekker will do, but Lawrence will not.

In *Mornings in Mexico* we look in vain for the volcano gods of Aztec lore or for the customs of Tula and Culiacan. The fat reeds growing in the waters of Timilco which were offered to Xilonen are not in the book, nor do we find the goddess of maize, or Ciucoatl, the she-evil who brings men poverty, misery, the digging-stick and the tump-line. Lawrence has no words for the month of Mac when the turtles lay their eggs, or for Xul the time the fish spawn. There is no record of Teteu innan, the Mother of the gods, or of Opochtli, patron deity of the fisher.

Legend is the bread of the people, but we are hungered; our past is as unknown as the cemetery of the jaguar and the mastodon in the Andes. Our forefathers have disappeared, and we feign that we can begin NOW and be wise. We are dying because we do not even know how to feed ourselves; we have slain the stone pestle for pounding the honey; we have murdered the rocks, and we cannot hear the fogs that tarry in the peaks of Cacatepec. Our books are the waifs of the Muses, there is no mother or father or marriage-bed in them.

What profit has a man of his head, asks the primitive. The mind is not as large as the foot, the hand, or the ten toes, and far less trustworthy. The ancient Egyptian embalmer passed the brain through the nostrils of the deceased. Agamemnon, instead of finding fault with himself, blamed the soothsayer Calchas for never having prophesied anything good for him. But he who trusts his blood is stubble and chaff in the wind, and knows not where he is to be driven. The blood is deceitful and unstable, and it changes its shape as often as lust, avarice, sloth, vanity and stupidity beckon it to be the goat, the swine, or the ass.

# *on* D. H. LAWRENCE: 3

DEAR HERBERT:

It seems to me that the modern novel about love is all dross and no Helen. Love is an abundant rejoicing, and the wit loves best; the poet regards his beloved as Ptolemy imagined the unknown hemisphere: her skirts are a great sphere to be circumnavigated with all the zeal of Magellan.

Caliban, heavy, morose matter, cannot be healed save by fable, wisdom or sorrow, and though gall and hyssop may deepen the poet's line, it is Ariel, the saucy sprite, who causes the melons and the vines to laugh, and who dimples the stones of Golgotha. The vestal is now more of Gorgon rock: the foolish virgin has disappeared from literature. In D. H. Lawrence, the amorist of our century, all the virgins are wise, and with plenty of oil in their lamps with which to find a gypsy, or a Sicilian.

The amorous poet is as chaste as Pythagoras' niece who removed her petticoat when she desired to cast aside her modesty, but put it on again when she wished to be demure. The wit rejoices in the knowledge that the doughty Scythian bowstring was made of the pudendum of the camel; man is also admonished by the same beast that privily retires to the desert to copulate. Whereas Ovid laments his concupiscent verse, Herrick, living mild on herbs and pulse, need not. No dearer singer in English is there than Herrick, and what in another shakes the nerves or gives us the squeamish fit is, in this poet, at the worst, penury in Arcadia:

> Give us then an Ant to eate;
> Or the cleft earee of a Mouse
> The abdomen of the Bee.

You recall, Herbert, the famished D. H. Lawrence matrons who have no other priapic diet than a Celtic, Swedish, or American noddy. In "The Woman Who Rode Away," the wife, a hard, predacious Saxon, is married to an American mining engineer, who covets her person, but she does not want him. "Darkly" hankering for the red glowing bodies clad in white cotton drawers, she mounts her horse to go to seek the old Aztec god, Quetzalcoatl, sprung of rain and dust. She meets a small covey of Indians chewing tortillas and drinking water out of a gourd, the sight of which stirs in her a primal vibration; she longs to be ravished: "Would they attack her now?" Unfortunately, they regard her without a jot of lust; she is a "giant, female white ant," of an alien, impermeable race, and quite inedible, sexually. One of the party, a "darkling" Indian, in a white shirt gathered into a loin-cloth, and of ruddy, pottery legs, takes hold of the horse's bridle, and they lead her to a remote pueblo.

Lawrence only cared to do nude figures; he put clothes on the men and women in order to remove them. He undressed women so that he could cast them to the Aztec knives very much as Poe stuffed the two spinsters up the chimney in the Rue Morgue. A primitive feminist, he wanted the garments to be dropped according to ancient Toltec rituals; the shoes had to be shed as maize was husked, the dress peeled away like the skin of the piñon nut. When the Saxon matron comes to the pueblo two old Indians, with sacrificial, obsidian knives, slit her boots and raiment which fall away until she is naked. In December she is denuded once more and brought before an ancient Cacique who touches her with his curried finger tips, but there is no desire in the hands, heavy with death and the mountains. Later, she is given a long, hypnotic Indian massage; the red masseurs drop sweet-scented oil on her limbs, back and sides, and then carry her in a litter to a place where she is sacrificed to the sun and to Tlaloc, the rain-god. Had Lawrence read this tale by another author he would have wryly said, "For heaven's sake, why doesn't some one attack the poor dear?"

I believe that Lawrence gulled his female readers no less than Whitman whose *Leaves of Grass* aroused the most tender love in Mrs. Gilchrist, an English widow, who came to America to be near the bard. But Whitman was a virgin Hippolytus, and Mrs. Gilchrist a Phaedra, who, having no satisfaction from her passion, wreaked her furies on myrtle leaves.

In Lawrence there is only one sex, the male, the woman is the negative part of Adam, and man, like the Aristophanic grasshopper, sows his seed in the ground. It is not Eve or the Shulamite for whom Lawrence trembled, but Apollo binding his hair in a fillet.

Herbert, have you the fortitude to reread these books? My own brain is an ember too feeble to keep me warm long enough to finish many of these novels and stories.

The captain in "The Prussian Officer" spends his flame upon his orderly, and in *The Plumed Serpent* Don Ramon and Cipriano are the children of Ham. Lawrence writes, "The two men embraced, breast to breast, and for a moment Cipriano laid his little blackish hands on the baked shoulders of the bigger man, and for a moment was perfectly still on his breast." Lawrence brings the rams and the turtle-doves of Moloch to male love. The amorous pangs of Ramon are for his friend: "with Cipriano he was most sure . . . even when they embraced each other with passion." The women repel him: "their soft, untidy, black hair, which they scratched for lice," "their never-washed feet and ankles . . . somewhat reptillian under the long, flounced soiled cotton skirt," and again, "the women were little and insidious." Juana, too, has "untidy hair, and a limping way of walking."

The women are brachs; Kate Leslie, in *The Plumed*

*Serpent,* staled by widowed sheets, craves a mestizo, the only gutwort for her lusts. The wife in "The Woman Who Rode Away" has appetites that Erebus cannot wither, and the Marchesa in *Aaron's Rod* is elderly, prehensile flesh. The young wife in the story, "Sun," goes naked to tempt the Italian gardener, but Lawrence, always Narcissus among the hibiscus flowers, is the one that is wooed.

Unlike Michelangelo, who cared only for masculine nudes, Lawrence had not the power to create massive figures; Ham's shame he knew, but he was unable to work with large, elemental energies, good or evil. Dawn and twilight are not colossi but agreeable watercolor drawings in Lawrence's books. Anaxagoras may declare that the sun is a rock no larger than Peloponnesus, but man is awed by so much territory. In myth the petticoat of Megara, the wife of Hercules, is vast; men and women mingle as daybreak and night. Thistles, maggots, osiers are titanic in legend because man must contend with God and the Kosmos. Lawrence ached for the Toltec, and the old god-lusts of the Aztec, for a reborning of the ritual of seed time and marriage; he pulsed for ancient beginnings, for the purlieus of Erech, and he trod the modern cities and habits and life in the winepress of his anger.

The immense, naked David of Michelangelo is a hymn of male love; Florence is a "man's town" in *Aaron's Rod,* but Lawrence could not transfigure his Shame, or utter it in a parable. The poet requires a tragic conception of size to create the vast matrix of Cybele, the huge thorax of David or a columnar Ham or Og. Time and space in Lawrence are a loathly quantum of matter, the result of inertia and the detritus of details. The lesser poet translates primal Nothing into time and space; the sage changes it into Wisdom: there are Void, God, Prometheus, Satan, Chance, and the worms that weave and sing at the mortal loom. The poet must hatch a pismire or a Jerusalem or an American Continent, just as it was fabled, according to Voltaire, that the descendants of Noah were brought to bed of giants near the Straits of Magellan.

Bacchus, Poseidon, Ocean are Kosmical Fathers; the Logos, Elohim, or the Demiurge labor to wrest from the great Primal Nothing a Plenum, for in the beginning was the Void.

Swift created the Lilliputian to show the littleness of men, but he gave us Gulliver to indicate the epic dimensions of humanity; he eats, walks and passes water prodigiously. No author should reveal habits or revulsions which enfeeble the reader as in Kafka's *Metamorphosis*. "Not weigh'd or winnowed by the Multitude, But swallow'd in the Mass, unchewed and crude," is from John Dryden's *Absalom and Achitophel*. Legend will help hold back queasiness; how many would not have a troubled stomach at the mention of Heliogabalus's urinal were it not wrought of the Unicorn?

Lawrence was no Daedalus of the novel; his books are glutted with adjectives which bring about the "prejudicial delay of the noun," as Lessing observed. Helen, as the ancients knew, can be imagined, but not described. In *Orlando Furioso* Ariosto writes: "She was in person so well formed as not to be depicted but by skilled painters." Horace asserted that "pure Description held the place of Sense."

There are many things that are true which are not facts and cannot be proven, as the story that Rouen was devastated by a winged dragon at the time of St. Romain. Plutarch believed that the Sphinxes, Chimeras, and Centaurs were real. What is absolutely unprovable is poetry; only the churl and the gutter-blood guttle the legends, but bow down before the Golden Calf and the Fact, the Proof and the Lie.

Myths were the viaticum of Aristotle's old age. The image and the fable are almost forsaken in the cold, deflowered *Laws* of Plato. Pompey was so affected by the fate of Prometheus that he asked the Greeks to show him where the god had been fettered by Zeus. In symbolic literature St. James the Elder is represented with the scallop shell, water bottle and staff, indicating that he was the pilgrim; St. James, brother of Jesus, is shown on stained glass, or in Christian sculpture, with the fuller's pole by which he was martyred. When the fable is sere and the symbols have died, the prophetic books are shut, and matter, wind and nard take the place of proverbs, epitaphs and worms. "You never know yourself till you know more than the body," wrote Traherne.

The epicure of the word is not a myth-maker. Flaubert took the legend of St. Julian, and Lawrence gave us a seminal Jesus, but neither conceived an apologue. The agonies of Julian are the wild apples of the senses. Julian has the appetite of the pard and leaps at the smell of the droppings of stags; he carries within him the malignant fate of Orestes. However, the *Orestes* of Sophocles is a great parable whereas "St. Julian" is an art-tragedy. Flaubert, like Silenus in the garden of Midas, was overcome by the fragrant flowers of his own genius. He cared more for the simile or the metaphor than he did for the Mount of Olives. What was holy for Flaubert was tone, milieu, the letter that killeth the legend and the spirit.

Flaubert's "St. Julian" is done with a sorcerer's knowledge, and yet it lacks the woe of dust and spirit. In the visionary the thing is the demon, and the thought the cherub. The objects in the world are confusion and misery and are as beasts that embowel man unless he has a tutelary Angel within him.

When the gods are dead the Muses are anile and their hymns are sung by Nestors with children's heads. Not only have the gods disappeared, but the camelopard, the kite and the heron have vanished from Mount Ida, and the brutes of the earth are important for men who require the symbolic life.

Myth is the source of poetry and he who does not believe, as Thomas Nashe held, that "the Salamander with his very sight blasteth apples on the trees," has a Gorgon Medusa in his entrails so that whatever he writes is stone, and what he sings has an ophidian hiss.

In *The Man Who Died* Christ is far less pagan than those fourteenth century Christians who worshipped the shift of the Virgin Mary and the prepuce of Jesus. After Lawrence's Christ has left the tomb he comes upon a gaudy, flaming rooster whose phallic crowing awakens in him the understanding of seminal particulars. Then Mary Magdalene recognizes him, though the bitterness of the Golgotha nails, the sere-cloth and corroding messiahship have brought sunset upon his flesh. He is middle-aged, heavy with the nausea of apathy, and he says to Magdalene, "Do not touch me, I am in death."

But Jesus is Thamuz for whom the women of Israel wept at the walls of Jerusalem; he is also Osiris whose limbs, torso, and testicles have been cast into the Nile by Typhon. This is not a story of the Brook Kidron, but a little tale about the doves of lust.

The rooster Jesus hears when quitting the sepulchre is not the one which announced the three betrayals of Peter, nor is this the Christ with the ass's head in the catacombs. The homilies belong to the terrible, pneumatic evenings of the young saviour, but the seminal Jesus hates the parables; "The fig tree can be barren if it will"; he renounces the vigils, the fasts and the hurts that press down upon the soul until it cries out its vision. Could not Jesus have kept the wondrous apothegm about the tares and the wheat, even though he has desires? Is it not wrong to deprive him of his destiny, and to hide his last words, "Abba, Abba, it is finished," which are in every great thought and act of mortals? Fire, air, earth and water suffer. Banish suffering and the elements become our Nemesis.

There is the temple of Isis, a wooden "lotus-bud of Egypt" attended by a vestal who comes out of the portals thrusting "one thigh forward through the frail fluting of her robe." "She is in anguish of bereavement of search," like the woman who rode away to the Indian pueblo.

In Anacreon Eros is a whirlwind descending upon the oaks, but in Lawrence the god is just small, libidinous excitement accompanied by some droll similes, as, "the very flower of her womb . . . was . . . like a bud in shadow of frost." Or, "He untied the string on the linen tunic, and slipped the garment down, till he saw the white glow of her white gold breasts. And he touched them, and he felt his life go molten. 'Father!' he said, 'why did you hide this from me?' "

Lawrence gave most of his mind to the delights of the flesh which are as short-lived as the season of grass. What could he hope of Aphrodite who forsook Montaigne and the poet of the *Sonnets*? It is perilous to remark that anyone can be harmed by others. It may be that his genius was his flaw, for human identity is an unalterable ore.

Forgive me, Herbert, as I again quote Kierkegaard who said, "Genius is a sin." What else are such titles as

*A Season in Hell* and *Les Fleurs du Mal* but gospels of vice. "Morality is the weakness of the brain," wrote Rimbaud. Is it not troublous to realize that most of our poets dwell in Purgatory and long to be somniferous insects, or dead. "I envied the felicity of beasts, caterpillars that represent the innocence of limbo, moles, the sleep of virginity . . ." (Rimbaud.)*

* Trans. by Louise Varèse, New Directions.

## *on* D. H. LAWRENCE: 4

DEAR HERBERT:

You write in one of your volumes that justice is a better word than morality; but shall we put good and evil, false and true in an expurgated index because they are so often the pompous shibboleths of Philistia? Are there not as many fat, pragmatic porkers in Bohemia as in Gaza?

He who eats of the Tree of Knowledge must judge. If one is a nihilist, or nearly so, as I am, there is still no other choice. Either we submit to the despotism of matter, or partake of the Tree of Good and Evil, which is the sublime food of Logos, that awakens the angels in our faculties.

Ruskin once described Rossetti's faults as "Moral insolences and iniquities." I doubt that a good man can be found in bad prose. The homiletical novels of Henry James deprive me of will and hope, and his unmanly sentences give me the ague all day long. What good is his didactic scorn for the shrewd Pallas Athene who holds the trident in one hand, and the ledgerbook in the other, if his prose so distresses my gorge that I can hardly keep it from coming up? The right words in the proper places is literature, as Swift said, and such skill is morality, and what Philister will give a shilling for it? Do you agree, Herbert, or not?

There is always the dragon's tooth in a poor book, though he who sowed it imagines that he was a great artist. Our books are as nude as Adam. Who is not ashamed of the last poem he wrote, or has not boundless cause for concealing himself from the book he has just finished, and crying out with the mortification of Adam, "I was naked, and I hid"?

I return to D. H. Lawrence whose novels will be no more than the cinders of Ilium in another fifty years. Maybe he will survive in another poet as Troy still exists in the *Iliads*.

The *Studies in Classical American Literature* are analects, good, wry talk. Before Lawrence American books on the poetasters in the American wilderness, Anne Bradstreet, the pamphleteer-versifier Freneau, and the gothic dunciad Brockden Brown, came from the dreariest academic scriveners. There was not a critical volume from which one could quarry a truth until Lawrence's *Studies* which seeded the works of Sherwood Anderson, Allen Tate, Hart Crane, William Carlos Williams's *In The American Grain* and Josephine Herbst's *The Hunter of Doves*.

Lawrence was thought to hate a democratic commonwealth. The truth is that he saw as little in the republic to kindle arcadian hopes as did de Tocqueville or Amiel.

He considered it most specious to affirm that the crabbed
Pilgrim fathers came to the New Continent for religious
freedom; anyone looking into some of those apoplectic
religious treatises of colonial America will hardly believe that the New England planter craved liberty. Anne
Hutchinson was sent into the wild forests after the Anti-
nomian trial, and in that plague which Nathaniel Ward
called *The Simple Cobbler of Aggawam,* he testifies that
he detests toleration and "forrainers." Even Roger Williams, who could not abide the stygian Mathers, was unable to endure a Quaker.

The Puritans ran away from the England of Spenser,
Marston, Lyly, Jonson; they left the land of the cavalier
bibliophile, King Charles, admirer of Andrew Marvell,
to live on sea-snails, mussels, pompions, gourds, and bear
suet. Lawrence announces three truths: that the American commonweal was from the beginning ruled by
beadles and shut church heads; that New England was a
fell refuge for adventurers, freebooters, self-sown Bible
citizens, and that the nature screed, spawned by Rous-
seau, was a fungused humbug.

Lawrence regarded the New World as a "negative
energy," and it is true that America is a wild, nether
force; the Pilgrims regarded themselves as planters, but
as one of them remarked, the Massachusetts vineyard
was a "New-Found Golgotha." There was not a single
domestic animal in Mexico when Cortes arrived; Colum-
bus imported the horse and the brood mare into the
Antilles; De Soto brought the first sows to Florida. The

Conquistadore, coming from the most polite nation in Europe, became, himself, a primitive, regarding a dog as much of a delicacy as a pheasant.

American literature is feral geography, non-human and elemental rather than didactic. The aboriginal books of the three Americas are beast gospels; in the Quiché Mayan tongue *balam* means sorcerer or jaguar. Baalim is an old Phoenician idol; Jesus was sometimes referred to by the learned rabbis as Baalam. The Quiché Maya call their sacred scripture *Chilam Balam,* which, like the New World, is a primeval brute psalm.

In the nineteenth century our sages were writing apocalyptic books about the albatross, leviathan, and the primordial, animal ground of New England. These volumes were congealed, Atlantic scriptures, intellectual short commons of eels and clams, and almost void of women. The French wived Indian women, the Spanish took them as concubines; the epic Viking manslaughterers, Eric the Red and Thorfinn the Skull-Cleaver, had natural issue and bedded lusty, female behemoths. But the Mathers gibbeted the Kate Hotspurs and Doll Tearsheets of Massachusetts.

Lawrence's chapters on Benjamin Franklin, Crèvecoeur, Fenimore Cooper, are either aphorisms of his own or diatribes against women. He says that all the characters in the Poe tales, Ligeia, Eleonora, Madelein Usher, and their lovers fornicate until they are exhausted and die. We leaped from the savage, anointing his skin with the oils of acorns, seething porridge with bruised elms and ash, to the rococo charnel-house of Poe, in less than two hundred years.

The *Studies* are often as sterile as the island of Scoria where amber grows! They are the first *Ecce Homo* book on American literature, which weaned us from the college presbyters on Whitman, Melville, Poe, Franklin. The modern plagiary has garnered wondrous sea-myth out of the chapter on *Typee* and *Omoo*. There were occasions when instead of using a mortal pen he blew the trump of the four angels. Close to Ocean, to the marine undercrust of man, he is a Thales or an Empedokles; it may be that like the early Greek cosmographers his fame will rest upon fragments:

> We are most of us, who use the English language, water-people, sea-derived.

> It must have once been a vast basin of soft, lotus-warm civilization, the Pacific. . . . Samoa, Tahiti, Raratonga, Nukuheva; the very names are a sleep and a forgetting.

> . . . the Pacific Ocean is aeons older than the Atlantic or the Indian Oceans. . . . Strange civilizations have convulsed the Atlantic and Mediterranean peoples . . . while the Pacific . . . peoples slept.

> Let water conceive no more with fire. Let mating finish. Let the elements leave off kissing, and

turn their backs on one another. Let the merman turn away from his human wife, and children, let the seal-woman forget the world of men, remembering only the waters.

Brown-eyed people are, as it were, like the earth, which is tissue of bygone life, organic, compound. In blue eyes there is sun and rain and abstract, uncreate element, water, ice, air, space, but not humanity.

### from *Apocalypse*

With the coming of Socrates and "the spirit," the cosmos died. For two thousand years man has been living in a dead or dying cosmos, hoping for a heaven hereafter.

The waters of the abyss were salt like the sea. Salt had a great hold on the old imagination. It was supposed to be the product of "elemental" injustice. Fire and water, the two great living elements and opposites, gave rise to all substance in their slippery unstable "marriage." But when one triumphed over the other, there was "injustice." So, when the sun-fire got too strong for the sweet waters, it *burnt* them, and when water was burnt by fire, it produced salt, child of injustice.

Vulcan took the hammer to bring forth Minerva from the head of Zeus; but Lawrence had not the strength for his genius. Was it then for lack of health that he was unable to understand the Colossus in art, to create an Adam, Seth, Prometheus, Satan, without which books are the villainy of the little?

It has been common to regard his work as the tiger with the flaming colors of Joseph's coat, but to cast the man into the ditch. When I was in diggings in London, sleeping until mid-afternoon so that I could sustain myself by one meal a day at a pub or from the tupenny meat-wagons, he sent me five pounds. He wrote me didactic, bullying letters which were accompanied by the two gudgeons and the barley loaves. I had not met the celebrated man, or given him any hint of those blighted London days. But hunger is a seraph, and though I regret many other torments in my life, I do not cast out indigence, my dearest teacher. We are eunuchs because we believe in money which can beget nothing. The epitaph of Thomas Churchyard is "Poetry and Poverty this tomb doth inclose."

I saw D. H. Lawrence for the first time at Sylvia Beach's bookshop in Paris; he had already written a preface for my first novel *Bottom Dogs*, receiving a pelting guerdon for his valiant work. I watched this lissomy man talking to Sylvia Beach, and for me he embodied the wild, rioting muses. He had a goatish jaw with beard, russet, earthed hair, and a potato nose. He looked like a Mayan idol, with beans for eyes and squash seeds for teeth—to use his own phrase, he was a crucified faun.

Some days later when we walked across the Boulevard Raspail I realized that the man was dying in his clothes. I had to help this spirited forty-three-year-old nature, for he was that rather than just a writer, to his room at the Hotel Grand Versailles.

He was the most moral man of his age, and he never ceased advising me to be the bony Spartan. He urged me not to let publishers cozen me of my lentils, and I never have because they never gave me any. He also counseled me not to be unlucky and said that I should always write with a great bitterness. Has it not been told that rage was the inventor of Archilochus' Iambic? I heeded his advice as best I could, for I have been a bitter stylist, and I have always been luckless. For all his fame, which he thought a disgrace, he replied to my letters at once. Being a genius he was alone, needing even my callow epistles without sun, wheat, grapes and rain. He quoted La Bruyère who said that all our miseries come from not being able to be alone. Delacroix sighed: "I wrote for myself alone." I say: "I write and am alone."

It was I who left off writing to him because I was ashamed of the empty, Cana words I sent to him. Of his person I can repeat what Lord Bolingbroke asserted of Bacon, "He was so great a man that I do not recollect whether he had any faults or not." Idol-breaking is seeing what we did not perceive in our purblind youth; unchanging yea-saying is stagnant water; for those who do not continually reject their former ikons and ideas are always children. Though I have altered my thoughts regarding his gifts, let it be my portion when I retire to Erebus to have as companions the disembodied dust of Hesiod, Homer, Musaeus, Apollo and D. H. Lawrence. "Eat and carouse with Bacchus," Lawrence says, "or munch dry bread with Jesus, but don't sit down without one of the gods."

## *on* D. H. LAWRENCE: 5

DEAR EDWARD:

You have dealt so thoroughly with Lawrence's ambiguous eroticism that I need say no more on the subject—except this: that it is not only his female readers who are gulled: the adolescent youth too will warm to this exclusive maleness. We are all bi-sexual, and one might say that the division of primitive Man-Woman, as related by Aristophanes in Plato's "Symposium," was physical only: the psychic gender is still composite and still a threat to the gods. It is odd that Lawrence never seems to have realized the presence or the potency of this *anima* that haunted his mind; but it is the key to his twisted sexuality.

Deep within himself he always hungered for a reunion of the sexes, and Love was for him, as it was for Plato, the "desire and pursuit of the Whole." He gave another name to this desire and pursuit—not love, but "true relatedness." It is the central doctrine of all Lawrence's work. The best definition of it comes from an essay with the significant title "Morality and the Novel" (*Phoenix*, pp. 527–32):

If we think about it, we find that our life *consists in* this achieving of a pure relationship between ourselves and the living universe about us. This is how I "save my soul" by accomplishing a pure relationship between me and another person, me and other people, me and a nation, me and a race of men, me and the animals, me and the trees or flowers, me and the earth, me and the sky and sun and stars, me and the moon: an infinity of pure relations, big and little, like the stars of the sky: that makes our eternity, for each one of us, me and the timber I am sawing, the lines of force I follow; me and the dough I knead for bread, me and the very motion with which I write, me and the bit of gold I have got. This, if we knew it, is our life and our eternity: the subtle, perfected relation between me and my whole circumambient universe.

And morality, he adds, "is that delicate, forever trembling and changing *balance* between me and my circumambient universe, which precedes and accompanies a true relatedness."

All Lawrence's work—novels, poems and essays—is to be seen as an effort to achieve this "true relatedness." More than that: as you read his letters (as a coherent body of writing, perhaps his greatest literary achievement) you see that the whole of his life, his loves and hates, his restless traveling, his attempts at painting and his plans for a "colony"—all are part of his pathetic desire and pursuit of the Whole, a wholeness not of man and woman only, but of Man-Woman with the circumambient universe, the Heaven of the Gods.

It is in this general context of "true relatedness" that he conceived the "sex thing," as he inelegantly called it. That, too, was a question of true relatedness. Alas, nothing in his work is so dreary and tasteless, so fumbling and artless, as this doctrinaire approach to the subtle realities of human relationships. When Zeus, in Plato's myth, divided the primordial creature, he used very delicate methods, "as one cutteth apples for pickling, or eggs with hairs." Lawrence thought he could re-unite the two parts with a rope of brutal words. I believe him when he says that his only desire is "to make an *adjustment in consciousness* to the basic physical realities." But in this matter we cannot make too many allowances for Lawrence's innocence—for his boundless provincial naïveté, for his disarming lack of sophistication. (He knew what sophistication was, however, and he avoided it.) He really thought, as he said in a letter to Lady Ottoline Morrell (28 December, 1928) that "the common people," who are notoriously inept in sexual matters, had a more perfect relation to sexual realities because they could use, without affectation, "without a shudder or a sensation," words like piss and shit. He did not realize (as any educated man who has served in the army is soon made to realize) that "the common people" do not use these words *with any meaning at all*. They don't shudder when they use them for the very good reason that they are merely uttering senseless expletives, and to talk as Lawrence did of "the good natural glow of life" (and he means sexual life) among such people is just sentimental nonsense.

Sex, like every other aspect of life, is just as beastly or as angelic as we make it. There exists an identity here which Lawrence did not recognize or appreciate. The beast and the angel have a single shape. But let me be more explicit. Lawrence pitied Swift—"think of poor Swift's insane *But* of horror at the end of every verse of that poem to Celia. But Celia shits!—you see the very fact that it should horrify him, and simply devastate his consciousness, is all wrong, and a bitter shame to poor Celia." But if Lawrence is referring to "The Lady's Dressing-Room," where the phrase occurs (it is repeated in "Cassinus and Peter") then he is misreading Swift. The words in question come at the climax of the poem. And how does the poem then proceed? In a way that illustrates my point. Strephon, who has been peeping into the lady's dressing room, receives this shock, and is then punished for his peeping:

> His foul imagination links
> Each dame he sees with all her stinks . . .

and *he*, says Swift, is the man to be pitied; and he concludes:

> Should I the Queen of Love refuse,
> Because she rose from stinking Ooze?

To him that looks behind the Scene
*Satira*'s but some pocky Quean.
If *Strephon* would but stop his Nose . . .
He soon would learn to think like me,
And bless his ravisht Sight to see
Such Order from Confusion sprung,
Such gaudy Tulips rais'd from Dung.

There is nothing very "insane" about such a conclusion—in fact, it is a triumph of reason or common-sense, or perhaps of intuition. Reason compels us to recognize the carnal facts; reason also should compel us to acknowledge the transcendent nature of love. Intuitively we may then hit upon the truth that these two realities are not unrelated: that the spirit thrives on the flesh, the tulip on the dung. Lawrence protests against "the awful and truly unnecessary *recoil*" from the facts, and says it is only a question of "conscious acceptance and adjustment." But Swift did not recoil from the facts, nor did he self-consciously isolate them for acceptance. He observed that a miracle was involved—that a tulip had grown from the dung. He accepted the tulip, for its grace and beauty, and did not think it necessary to spoil his enjoyment by conscious thoughts about its roots. Surely Lawrence had forgotten Swift's "true (and "pure") relatedness" to Stella—not an "adjustment," but one of the most natural and enduring attachments in the history of human passion.

One comes back again and again, in all observations

on the prerequisites of beauty in art, to the necessity for "distance." "Distance is the soul of the beautiful" (Simone Weil). A pure relationship "between me and another person, me and other people, me and a nation, me and a race of men, me and the animals," etc.; yes—an infinity of pure relationships, but let them be relationships "like the stars of the sky," the stars that are kept at infinite distances from one another by laws that are universal. All art involves an act of contemplation: *not* the kind of active involvement that Lawrence demands, which is also the demand of the Expressionists in the plastic arts; but "a carnal attraction which keeps us at a distance and implies a renunciation." Simone Weil again, who goes on: "The beautiful is that which we desire without wishing to eat it (a fruit which we look at without trying to seize it). We desire that it should be. We have to remain quite still and unite ourselves with that which we desire yet do not approach."

Lawrence held strongly to one half of the truth about beauty and about love (and perhaps about life and death, being and non-being). He realized that "Eternity is only an abstraction from the actual present. Infinity is only a great reservoir of recollection, or a reservoir of aspiration: man-made. The quivering, nimble hour of the present, that is the quick of time. This is the immanence. The quick of the universe is the *pulsating, carnal self,* mysterious and palpable. So it is always."

This realization gave urgency to Lawrence's writing whenever he contemplated the objective world of flowers and plants, of animals and birds: the utterance was then "like a spasm, naked contact with all the influences at once. It does not want to get anywhere. It just takes place."

In those rare moments Lawrence was a poet, united with what he contemplated. But only for an instant. Then he began to want to get somewhere—began to talk of conscious acceptance and adjustment. And so we get his crude gamekeeper, trying to put the upper classes right, trying to adjust them to his mutton chop view of sex. The spell was broken. The fruit that should have been contemplated was eaten. The crystal consciousness was clouded by moral purpose. There was no perfect work of art.

But now I come back to my first assertion—that Lawrence has been the greatest writer of our generation (I use the word "generation" deliberately, to separate him from Henry James, who belongs to an earlier generation). The word "writer" is also ambiguous: I do not mean poet or novelist, and to call him a moralist is to suggest that he is no kind of artist at all. His nearest "comrade" is Whitman, about whom he wrote an essay that is possibly the best he ever wrote—inspired by perfect understanding and sympathy. Whitman is usually considered a poet, a great poet, but as I have argued elsewhere (*The True Voice of Feeling*), he is a poet of a peculiar kind, not metrical so much as grammatical, not lyrical but rhetorical. Lawrence is exactly the same kind of poet. Some of his poems, like "The Ship of Death," are close imitations of Whitman; but his best poems are hidden in his prose, from which they could be abstracted, as you have abstracted fragments in your last letter, and these fragments could be arranged like Whitman's *Leaves of Grass*, or like Jeremiah's prophecies. Extract all such poems from Lawrence's novels ("an insulting suggestion," says Mr. Angus Wilson), and we should have a body of work not incomparable to Whitman's. And what would be left? Nothing but chaff— polemical dummies stuffed with straw, mutton chops and mugs of beer.

These poems, which would not be true poems like the poems of Shakespeare or Keats, but dithyrambic utterances, would cry out in the wilderness of our newsprint, like a great prophetic challenge to our civilization. And in the end one could say, as Lawrence said of Whitman, that he was a great leader, a great changer of the blood in the veins of men.

And one might admit, above all our distinctions of art and morals, of poets and prophets:

"The only riches—the great souls."

on HENRY JAMES

## *on* HENRY JAMES: 1

DEAR HERBERT:

Henry James was as debilitated in his books as Pope was in life; the latter could scarce stand on his feet, while the former, perspiring over his syntax, sends those he tortures to Egyptian ideographic writings in which a pair of legs going denotes the transitive verb.

The rueful decline of diction in literature "presses down upon my identity," to cull a phrase from Keats. The idols in England and America are trade, the howling of the triple-throated Cerberus called the radio, the newspaper, and the repulsive pleasure in mangling language which is similar to the joy Emperor Domitian derived from unwinging flies with a bodkin. Homer employed archaisms to reinvigorate Greek which had dropped since the time Cadmus had brought the Phoenician alphabet to Thebes. There is no mutton or bread or ale in modern English: a poor, sere whore, her chin hangs, and her wanton plackets entice neither Anthony Dull nor Master Dotage.

The modern author does not plead his cause with Waller, or Skelton, or Langland or Chaucer, but instead turns to that cockatrice of modern nations, the newspaper, which has hatched words that send the imagination to the vomitories. Coleridge had suggested that there ought to be an Index Expurgatorious of worn-out phrases and banalities.

To return to Henry James, what can you glean from the *Prefaces* except the knowledge that the author was the sovereign of the enervated phrase, who dropped his reader's blood on the Mount of Olives? After Defoe and Smollett what a falling off there is in the affected alliterations, the repetitions of the same word which give dramatic emphasis to a luminous vacuity: "Mrs. Gereth was, obviously, with her pride and her pluck, or an admirable fine paste," ". . . this young man must either have had less of the principle of development to have had so much of the principle of collapse, or less of the principle of collapse, to have had so much of the principle of development," ". . . without intensity where is vividness, and without vividness where is presentability?" When Immanuel Kant was asked to explain his philosophy, the eighty-four-year-old sage replied that he meant what he had said, and that, moreover, he had more important things to do than to write a commentary on his works.

No author in the republic of letters has had a more tragic fear of his occupation than Henry James. Before sitting down to write, Henry James waited for the haruspex to inspect the entrails to see whether the signs were favorable for the composition of a novel. He approached his task with the vast misgivings of a Brutus preparing to go to battle, and the author, no less than the Roman stoic, heard his Evil Genius say, "We shall meet at Philippi."

When one has the nervous irritabilities of the artist without the strength to handle the brazier and the tools of the Titans, he has the vibrant soul of an upholsterer or a delicate sempstress. James had so little masculine force that he had to take up the lady trades of the ruse, the advantage, and the investment. In the Preface to *The Ambassadors*, he compared the novelist's quest for his subject to a species of "matching, as the ladies say, at the shops, the big piece with the snippet." Coleridge wrote of those authors who had sacrificed the intellect to point and drapery. What Max Beerbohm once said of a venal American scribbler applies to this ill-fated, but devout votary of literature: "Poor Mr. James, he wanted so much to be an artist."

A devotee of style, he wrote superannuated, sighing sentences with a dull metronomic beat. He studied decorum so mercilessly that he knew whether the florid face of a hostess and her carpet jarred, or if she were morally booted, or her dress went with the Dresden objects of art. He believed in the moral properties of furnishings, for milieu was his passion. James accumulated his circumlocutions for design, because he cared more for propriety than he did for the universe. Everything he did was governed by taste, and it was impossible for him to be clear because he wanted to be sure and tactful.

Fussing over his sentences, putting in long, enervating parentheses, and adding double negatives to achieve the exact shade of meaning, he then tortured the poor, tired sentence all over again to make a positively arid and mediocre observation. He created a specious rhetoric which has since been taken up as literary grammar by the Jamesian acolytes.

The noise of the magpie is no more of a garrulous chatterer than James's prose. Ford Madox Ford, who admired Henry James, wrote an affectionate parody on his mannerisms, and what Ford called "the later convolutions of epithet": "So that here, not so much locally, though to be sure we're here, but at least temperamentally in a manner of speaking, we all are." This is Henry James writing: ". . . the conscious sinking, at all events, and the awfully good manner, the difference, the bridge, the interval, the skipped leaves of the social atlas—these, it was to be confessed, had little, for our young lady, in default of stouter stuff, to work themselves into the light literary legend—a mixed, wandering echo of Trollope, of Thackeray, perhaps mostly of Dickens—under favour of which her pilgrimage had so much appealed." ". . . yet she also made out that if they had all consciously lived under a liability to the chill breath of *ultima Thule* they couldn't, either, on the facts, very well have done less." When he was not diffuse he was incorrigibly banal: "The idea was bright, yet the girl but beautifully stared," "jaunty males or as ostensibly elegant women," "the tall, rich, heavy house

at Lancaster Gate," "Kate was a prodigious person. . . ."
The opposite of genius, said Paul Valery, is diffusion.

James imagined that effete, exchequer breeding could
save him from vulgarity and libidinous shock, and he selected ordinary society people of England as composition wallpaper, quatorze furniture, and the debile smile
at five o'clock tea which concealed adultery, cant and
avarice. What was important was not to show any fault
barbarously, or near sordid crockery or a vulgar settee.
He wrote: "The worst horror was the acres of varnish."

James loathed poverty. Being poor meant having a
cheap, penny fate; art to James was a bribe offered to the
gods. Once when Ford brought a guest, who the old man
at Rye thought was of low origin, he refused to receive
him. The poor could never be put in the right relation to
intrigue. He never forgave Gustave Flaubert for receiving him in Paris in a soiled *atelier* smock. What anxiety
he felt when he visited De Maupassant who had a demi-
monde in his room with nothing on but a mask.

The sole Jamesian principle is taste, not energy. The
matrons of portly suasions promote the ruse. The ma-
triarch in *The Golden Bowl,* though in middling circumstances, is accustomed to objects of genteel breeding,
and is suitable to be the mentor of nubile virgins and
wan, young men. Mrs. Touchett in *The Portrait of a
Lady* takes Isabel Archer away from Albany and sets
her where she may, by the finest shadings, move from
virginity to gentle, fiscal bridehood. In *The Golden Bowl*
it is the elderly Fanny Assingham upon whom the Prince

leans. Her husband is a doltish colonel who helps her provide a gelded marriage in which two people occupy staled, septic space without rough, sexual collision. Jamesian fiction is generally the same. The society women are kitchen Bridgets, and the suitors, ardent as slugs, are pseudo males; a masculine nature is coarse, confused flesh. The Prince is dull, or as James writes in one of his countless, high-born platitudes, "innocent, beautiful, vague." Owen Gereth in *The Spoils of Poynton*, the shabbiest piece of manhood, is attempting to escape two leonine matriarchs, Mona Brigstock, whose name suggests the worthy battle material of which she is composed, and his mother, who spoils the house at Poynton of its valuable, artistic furniture. With what penury of energy he has, Owen tries to get himself married to Fleda Vetch. That is entirely satisfactory to Mrs. Gereth, because she knows that she will be the curatorial mistress of the museum pieces at Poynton, and the still-life marriage will be no more than a part of the seemly, dead appointments.

There are two tragedies, the drama of interior decoration, and the tragedy that Owen has to be taken and that Fleda, meaning she has fled before she can be espoused, cannot gather him up to her. She has a double fatality in her name, Fleda Vetch; the vetch is a bean, and according to Pythagoras, too sacred to be eaten.

James was the canniest peeping male that ever observed feminine habits. In his lengthy, busybody sentences he is not behind the arras watching a woman; he is much too near her for that. In *The Golden Bowl,* when Charlotte Stant comes into the room and sees her hostess with a man whom she has not expected, she comes in altogether composed, which is just what a woman would do, and exactly what a man cannot do without being exorbitantly clumsy. Such trifling details are only valued by the feminine. James comprehends the female need to delay, and knows that patience is the shrewdest tactic of a woman, and also her malady (which is why she is a Jamesian pragmatist rather than a visionary); it is his knowledge of decorum that enables him to smell adultery in *The Portrait of a Lady.* When Isabel Archer notices her husband seated while he is talking to Mme. Merle, who is standing, she knows that the relaxed, intimate familiarity between them is illicit. We think Webster clever when the Duchess of Malfi reveals that she is pregnant by asking for an apricot, and we are as baffled as Troilus when salacious, wenchy Cressid is in the arms of Diomede in the Greek camp. But does Webster or Shakespeare know as much as a washerwoman who launders the seminal sheet of the profligate, or the he-or-she novelist, Henry James?

I do not blame Henry James so much for his defects, because I admire a zealous failure. It is the quacks of the lute and the harp, whose windy sounds pass off as literary canons, that I abhor. The Poet says, "Foolery, sir, does walk about the orb like the sun." Is it not, Herbert, our duty to advise the novice against the day of his own unearned fame? Goethe wished "to spare the

young those circuitous paths, on which he himself had
lost his way."

In the Preface to *The Spoils of Poynton*, Henry James
has asked, ". . . why then Fleda Vetch, why a mere
little flurried bundle of petticoats, why not Hamlet or
Milton's Satan?" It is a hapless quandary, but there is a
choice between the unprophetic dwarf of assets and lia-
bilities in the Jamesian novel, and Cybele, as Landor
says, "who carried towers and temples on her head."

The names of his termagants represent the weight and
persuasion of their hinder parts: Fanny Assingham, a
shrewish tautology, Maud Manningham, and Mrs. Brigstock, acres of shrewd buttocks, are as close as he comes
to Sir Toby Belch or Andrew Aguecheek. Aside from the
names of such dry, pecuniary beef, there is no anatomy
or wit in the novels. The male, like Ralph Touchett, as
his cognomen suggests, is too skittish and wan of bones
and mind. His heroines are stupid doves, for Milly
Theale, in *The Wings of the Dove* is no Semiramis, the
wild pigeon. There is no virgin in any of the books re-
sembling the females who, as Montaigne tells us, hid a
figure of the phallus in their caps when they came to the
windows.

James knew that money is the "great American seda-
tive." He was an artist in a phrase, trampled down in
those sterile tracts of nullity he titled novels. Dullness
is a lodestone and draws to it every simpleton. Those
who eulogize Henry James steal the praise that belongs
to others; besides bequeathing to an entire century a

cairn of confusion. Henry James was an exquisite mediocrity, and there is always insanity in what is average.

Give us venison, or the pulse and water of Herrick,
but I like my plate and cup of literature "well-lan-
guaged." If it's a vigil, or cold contemplation, I'll nour-
ish myself upon what you, Herbert, call the "marmoreal
epistles" of Samuel Daniel. Take jolly, learned companions, or fall upon your pen; the only criticism that
one may count upon in this world comes out of the
mouth of Falstaff: "Company, villainous company, hath
been the spoil of me."

## *on* HENRY JAMES: 2

DEAR EDWARD:

It seems that Henry James incites you to a revulsion that is almost physical. I am reminded of his own attitude to Conrad—"that monstrous master mariner" (Ford's story, and therefore probably apocryphal). You are revolted by his social snobbery, his cultivation of "taste," his epicene curiosity, and by something sexless and timid in his personal life. Well, I feel something of all this, too, but no author is perfect and some of our best poets have had mean natures (Shakespeare's testament does not suggest that he had a very generous or noble spirit).

But your charges are precise—you accuse James of effeteness of style and of a general lack of virility in his conception of character: you see him as an old lady confined to a sick-room, crocheting endless lengths of intricate lace. Worse than that—the old lady is a busybody, prying into the boudoirs she has never entered with a man!

It is still an argument *ad hominem*, and you do not substantiate your charges with any detailed analysis of

either the novels as such, nor of their style. As for the
man, I never met him, and have no personal feelings toward him; but I have known two or three people who
were close friends of his, and their devotion was absolute. I think you have only to read his letters, and the
two autobiographical books (*A Small Boy and Others*
and *Notes of a Son and Brother*) to feel yourself in the
presence of a man who had a large view of the world,
infinite discrimination, and passionate sympathy for the
saving graces. He was not heroic, in the overt sense, but
as a man and as an artist he must have suffered deep
humiliations. It would be absurd to call his life tragic,
but in the worldly sense it was never successful. He was
never a popular author, and only Flaubert and Zola have
suffered such direct insults (I am thinking of the first
night of his play, *Guy Domville*).

Admittedly his life suggests self-protection, retreat,
even a kind of cowardice. He loved Society better than
his fellow-men. There is a revealing letter which he
wrote to John Bailey, refusing the chairmanship of the
English Association—it was stupid to make such an
offer to such a man. In this letter he describes himself
as "a mere stony, ugly monster of *Dis*association and
Detachment," and defends himself in terms which I
think might appeal to you: ". . . the rough sense of it
is that I believe only in absolutely independent, individual and lonely virtue, and in the serenely unsociable
(or if need be at a pinch sulky and sullen) practice of
the same; the observation of a lifetime having convinced

me that no fruit ripens but under that temporarily grace-
less rigour, and that the associational process for bringing it on is but a bright and hollow artifice, all vain and
delusive." Perhaps I admire such detachment too wist-
fully, too enviously; but even if, in his case, resolution
followed all too closely on inclination, nevertheless it
was the integrity of the artist that he was defending, "the
sanctity and sufficiency of the life of art," as Percy
Lubbock calls it in his Introduction to the *Letters*. "It
was absolute for him that the work of the imagination
was the highest and most honourable calling conceivable, being indeed nothing less than the actual creation
of life out of the void."

It is the art and not the artist that you attack. But there
is so much you leave unsaid—the whole problem of
*form*, to Henry James no less important than the predominating *passion*, indeed, identical with it—this you
leave unmentioned. You give James no credit for what
was his life-long endeavour—to create a fictional form
as intense and as moving as the form of the classical
drama. "To work successfully beneath a few grave,
rigid laws . . .": that was his ideal. He worked relentlessly beneath these laws, and there is no fiction anywhere else in the world that comes near to the formal
perfection of his.

You have two objections to this claim: you say that the
form embraces no worthwhile substance, and that it is
accompanied by an inadequate, a trivial, a mediocre

style. Let me take this question of style first, for I feel most strongly about it.

James's style is idiosyncratic—it would be fatal to imitate it; it is not viable. Nor is Sir Thomas Browne's, or Laurence Sterne's, or Meredith's. A style may be personal or impersonal, to the degree that logic or feeling is predominant in it. James's style is personal, and the feeling that controls it is so subtle and fluctuant that it penetrates to coigns and into recesses that the bland light of logic never reaches. It is an infinitely complex style, and its intricacy is a quality we should admire, not condemn. It has been called "baroque," but that is not good enough. Baroque may stand for an empty forceful rhetoric, a mere façade to an empty building. James's style is rarely rhetorical in this sense: it is much more analytical, and permeates the whole substance of his thought. It is an infinitely modulated *voice*, and if it irritates you, you must suspect a temperamental aversion in yourself. Other people find it exquisite.

It is infinitely variable, too—from the sober Hawthornean simplicity of the early novels, through the sonorous majesty of the middle period, to the filigree intricacy of the final phrase. "A dull metronomic beat!" I can think of no more inappropriate charge. But before risking an example let me confess what you already know from my remarks on Lawrence's fictional style—that the whole business of describing people's actions and even people's thoughts—that the whole business of *imagining how* they act and behave, how they put down cups of tea and sit on chairs—all this strikes me in general as infinitely tedious and long-winded. The novel is a bourgeois substitute for the drama; and myth of any kind, for precision and permanence, demands the concentrated rhythms of poetry. I am therefore defending James's fictional style only within the conventions of fiction. But granted these one can open his books anywhere and find the instrument functioning efficiently. I will make the experiment. Here is *The Portrait of a Lady*, first published in 1880. I quote from the revised edition and the first volume opens at page 59. I read:

> It may be affirmed without delay that Isabel was probably very liable to the sin of self-esteem; she often surveyed with complacency the field of her own nature; she was in the habit of taking for granted, on scanty evidence, that she was right; she treated herself to occasions of homage.

It is bread-and-butter writing, but I do not find it dull or lacking in cadence; an image like "the field of her own nature" is lively and apt, and the last phrase is witty. But let us try the later style, that so offends even inveterate admirers of the mature James. Here is *The Wings of the Dove*, and again I open the book at random:

> These were immense excursions for the spirit of a young person at Mrs. Lowder's mere dinnerparty; but what was so significant and so ad-

monitory as the fact of their being possible? What could they have been but just a part, already, of the crowded consciousness? And it was just a part likewise that while plates were changed and dishes presented and periods in the banquet marked; while appearances insisted and phenomena multiplied the words reached her from here and there like plashes of a slow thick tide; while Mrs. Lowder grew somehow more stout and more instituted and Susie, at her distance and in comparison, more thinly improvised and more different—different, that is, from every one and every thing: it was just a part that while this process went forward our young lady alighted, came back, taking up her destiny again as if she had been able by a wave or two of her wings to place herself briefly in sight of an alternative to it.

Cannot you admire the hovering involutions of that last long sentence—like the flight of a bird against the wind? And again the images—"like plashes of a slow thick tide"; and the perfect aptness of the epithets—Mrs. Lowder, for example, growing more *instituted*? Again, I present it only within its fictional limits; but it is a little more interesting than Lawrence's beer-mug and mutton-chop style—not because the party was grander, but because there is a more subtle intelligence at work.

For the best of James's writing I would go to his let-

ters rather than to his novels, for there he is not irked
by the "exhibitory" needs of a fictional plot. I confess
that I can now read his letters with more pleasure than
his novels; and to these I would add the prefaces to the
novels, and the considerable body of critical and de-
scriptive prose he wrote. There are beautiful evocations
of scenes and places in his essays; and the whole of his
writing, I would say, is "charged with a *tone*, a full and
rare tone of prose," which is what he once said of Haw-
thorne's writing (in *Notes of a Son and Brother*), adding
that "this made for it an extraordinary value in an air in
which absolutely nobody else's was or has shown since
any aptitude for being." Tone is, of course, an intangi-
ble quality, but James's style has it, to a degree I cannot
see matched in any other modern English writer (Proust
has it in French). And to the tone of the style corre-
sponds the final, and perhaps the most significant quality
in his writing, its *moral* tone.

I have so often protested against the confusion of art
and morality that you will not suspect me of dragging
an old herring across the stage. The whole question of art
and morality, or of art and society, or of art and life
itself, is the degree of implicitness. If we have any faith
in life left in us, we should on that basis aspire to nobil-
ity, to goodness, to whatever ethical term we may adopt
for the continuous affirmation of life itself. But we do not
serve this cause by preachment, or by any direct inten-
tions on our neighbours. The moralist would say that we
serve by example, by unconscious habit. We, who are

not moralists, but artists, must make the same asseveration: the morality is implicit in the art, in the form and the style of it, finally in the impalpable tone of it. James realized this, no writer ever more clearly, and whatever his limitations as a creator of character (and the limits are of width, not depth), he is the chief exemplar in our time, and perhaps of all time, of the indispensable virtues of form—virtues, I reiterate, indispensable to feeling. There is a passage in his Introduction to *The Tragic Muse* where he makes this point superbly—let me end this letter by quoting it:

> A picture without composition slights its most precious chance for beauty, and is moreover not composed at all unless the painter knows *how* that principle of health and safety, working as an absolutely premeditated art, has prevailed. There may in its absence be life, incontestably, as "The Newcomes" has life, as "Les Trois Mousquetaires," as Tolstoi's "Peace and War" [*sic*], have it; but what do such large loose baggy monsters, with their queer elements of the accidental and the arbitrary, artistically *mean*? We have heard it maintained, we will remember, that such things are "superior to art"; but we understand least of all what *that* may mean, and we look in vain for the artist, the divine explanatory genius, who will come to our aid and tell us. There is life and life, and as waste is only life sacrificed and thereby prevented from "count-

ing," I delight in a deep-breathing economy and an organic form. My business was accordingly to "go in" for complete pictorial fusion, some such common interest between my first two notions as would, in spite of their birth under quite different stars, do them no violence at all.

No. Art, as you know, has its saints and martyrs, its prophets and evangelists, and for me Henry James has something in him of them all.

## *on* HENRY JAMES: 3

DEAR HERBERT:

Books are battles of the intellect, for which reason Longinus preferred the *Iliads* to the *Odyssey*. Feeble
writing is pusillanimous, for whoever deprives people
of light and health, Apollo and Aesculapius, is a cowardly sleeper who forgets his native earth.

When you write about Swift and Coleridge you observe the most chaste canons of literature, but sometimes
in dealing with our contemporaries you pass by the Lake
of Memory, as Plato says, and drink of the waters of
Lethe. You confess you cannot read James's novels any
longer with much pleasure. But does Homer wither your
palate? Do you reread Horace's *Odes* with less joy?
Does Chaucer slay your hopes, and will not another
perusal of Catullus's "Epithalamium" increase your
longings?

One can neither praise everything nor avoid blaming
those who are despoiling the entire world of its gold of
Ophir, its thinkers. August Vacqueries wrote ". . . Louer
tout, c'est une autre façon de denigrer tout."

You refer me to James's *Letters* but I still find the

same "studiously inverted" sentences as are in *The Ambassadors*. You have, of course, most of the literati on your side. But I cry out with Ben Jonson, "Opinion, O God, let gross opinion sink." When a man is weak in his novels he is not likely to be Hercules in his epistles.

The academic, too, will espouse your cause. Many so-called critics long ago envisaged the lucre to be had in avowing Henry James, the grandmother of the ladies' home novel. But then, Herbert, mob-appreciation is no cause for rejoicing. When you think of the illiterates who have been advocates of Joyce, Lawrence, Gide, James, Cocteau, you do not consider the lilies but the dunghill. All the nonsense about Joyce, Lawrence and James is pocketbook aesthetics. For an author to be well known today is a tacit avowal that he is a whore; for fame would appear to be a conspiracy against genius.

It was William Dean Howells, a mercenary prig, and the astute editor of the dead *Atlantic Monthly*, who gave James the idea for *The Ambassadors*. The author of *The Rise of Silas Lapham* is a cockatrice for any writer to behold or to imitate. One page of *The Ambassadors* is enough to sink all hopes and put out the fires which destroyed Ilium and created the *Iliad*. Lewis Lambert Strether, Waymarsh, and Bilham, "the little artist man," are feckless and fatigued. As Hazlitt remarked of another author ". . . all of his characters are tired of their lives, and you heartily wish them dead." I believe there is not even one line in the whole fiction that is not hackneyed.

The following are some of the typical inversions which should be balsam to the art-noodles of today. "She occupied, her hostess, in the rue de Bellechasse . . ." Despite the abnormal punctuation, it is our fervent orison that she did not occupy her hostess. Then again, there is James as the thinker: "The inwardness is a kind of inwardness that doesn't become an outwardness." He had, as he related, a "buxom muse" who had no thought of crawling into his fiction, which was a "vast formless feather-bediness." Is this really style and form?

Henry James never wrote a single virile page in his life. You regard him as a noble figure, but having no ability for his occupation he was not heroic enough to hold his tongue or his pen. A good line is often the result of chance; but James was always unlucky. He suffered from the malady of the word so much prated about in essays on Flaubert. This brings about a far worse disease than consumption, poult-foot, pleonasms, the ague, fungus, and the sickness that Dryden called synchysis, which is the ill-placing of words. Dionysius of Halicarnassus complains that Hegesias had so malignant a nature that even by accident he could not write one good sentence.

The male petticoat shows through James's letters as well; no one who is manly addresses a youth as though he were Cressid or Proserpine. It wears out the patience of any male who has to read James addressing a 'prentice novelist as "dearest, dearest Hugh," or "darling Hugh," and who can bear Whitman's infatuation for

Doyle, the conductor of a horse-car, without growing squeamish. When Zeus abducted Ganymede, this god was by then a lying Cretan, and not the bull mounting Europa.

Herbert, I age as I read his books, for there is no Aphrodite Ambologera, "She who staves off old age," in his novels. I doubt that those suety matrons and epicene male bipeds ever have any evacuations, for nobody in a James novel eats "the toasted flesh, and milk" of Chaucer. I would rather be humble *Silence* in the orchard eating his pippins and caraway seeds than be Henry James.

## *on* HENRY JAMES: 4

DEAR EDWARD:

I return, after an interval in which your silence
has expressed your dissatisfaction with my defense of
James, to a consideration of some general problems that
perhaps lie like a fog on the ground between us. You
are absolute for truth, and like a Grand Inquisitor,
would send to the stake any author who in any respect
offends your dogma. That dogma is not strictly aesthetic
—on the contrary, from the beginning of this correspondence you have spoken of virtue and health. Your
conception of the great writer is that of a sage or a seer,
a patriarch who instructs his people in a voice of authority, and castigates them with whips of scorn when they
are weak and errant. Your ideal author is Jonathan
Swift, whom you admire as much for his indignation as
for his style.

You find no *beau idéal* in our present age—all is
venality and corruption. Even Lawrence, who had some
perception of truth, lacked the strength for his genius.

I could not live so intolerantly. I am a relativist,
grateful for any glance of beauty that I encounter as I

read, and not anxious to erect monuments of granite on Parnassus. I am always for discrimination, which I would oppose to judgment. I love variety in a writer, even if it weakens his structure.

This is the usual romantic approach to literature, and I need not defend it at this stage of the history of criticism. But I am also a relativist in another sense, one that I shall not find easy to defend, especially in your court of judgment. I believe that the emotion which Keats experienced "on first looking into Chapman's Homer" is not repeated. There is a unique quality in the pleasure we feel on first reading any masterpiece of literature, and we return to such a masterpiece at our peril. At *our* peril, for the masterpiece does not change (except in so far as its language becomes obsolete); it is we who change, and the change is not necessarily toward an absolute standard of worth. We may know more as the years pass, but we feel less. It is not merely that our senses cloy: the "shock of recognition" does not repeat itself.

You challenge me to re-read the novels of Henry James. If I hesitate it is because I fear disillusionment rather than boredom or disapproval. This fear embraces every experience of the kind—I cannot pick up a play of Shakespeare's or Blake's poems without the same trepidation. I think there is only one novel in the whole of our literature that I have read more than twice—this is *Wuthering Heights*, and the reason I can always re-read this book has nothing to do with its literary qualities—

to explain the reason would be to explain myself. It is true that there are a few examples of "pure" poetry that seem to resist the staling of time—a few Elizabethan lyrics, Blake's Songs, two or three poems by Emily Brontë and Christina Rossetti—a mere handful of exceptions. But I know of no prose work that has this crystalline quality, though there may be a passage or two of Browne or Burnet or Boyle, even of Ruskin or Pater, that is crystalline in this sense, and there are many psalms and prayers that even the droning of a priest cannot kill. In this sense I could perhaps find a few passages from Henry James's prose that would bear repeated reading. But that is not the point at issue. It is the stature of James himself, as a novelist, as a master of narrative and as a portrayer of character, that you question.

You cannot stomach his style: I admit it is idiosyncratic. You cannot stomach his snobbery: I admit it is repellent. But I do not admit your main charge, that the sole principle he exhibits is taste, not energy. I find in his work two kinds of energy, both admirable—the energy of the constructive artist, the man who moulds his chosen instrument of expression to a clear conception of form and effect; and the energy of a moral sensibility, endlessly discriminating between shades of character and subtleties of behavior. You may not find these shades and subtleties of any great significance, and certainly James's heroes and heroines are not conceived on the scale of Greek or Elizabethan tragedy. But that is a virtue, for they are adjusted to our more microscopic vision. His tales are fables for our time, and his shrews and termagants, whom you find so skittish, can be met in any Anglo-Saxon home. His world is the prevailing, the predominating middle-class of his time, as authentic as the world of Chaucer, of Fielding, of Dickens. But it is also the same world, for though costumes and furniture change, the characters are essentially and humanly the same—Kate Croy is as solid as the Wife of Bath. Only the plots thicken—or if you prefer the image, proliferate—to exhibit a more sophisticated, a more corrupt, but authentically real society. It is not your society, it is not mine, but the moral issues are of our time, and if we have any imaginative sympathy at all (the same that we would give to the characters of a play by Shakespeare or even a Greek tragedy) we can enter into the plot and learn its lesson.

I re-read *The Wings of the Dove* eight years ago, for the specific purpose of writing an introduction to a new edition, and the final paragraph of that introduction will still stand as my final word on James:

> A moral tragedy cannot be epitomised: its excitement is in its subtleties of observation, its accuracy of discrimination, its accumulated perception of issues and dilemmas; and above all in the author's conscious control of the final issue. It might be objected that in this tragedy the heroine is not a victim claimed by exacting gods: she dies full of pity and forgiveness, and the retribu-

tion is left to work its poison in the consciences of the calculating lovers. We must admit that the pattern is not the classic one. But it would not have been like James to confine himself within such banal limits. Life itself does not conform to a traditional pattern, and it was life, in all its immediacy and contemporaneity, from which James drew his motives, and in which he could not honestly find the classical formula. But the effect is none the less cathartic; and when Milly dies we feel, if we have given the story the attention it demands, not perhaps that a great queen has gone to her doom, but rather that once more a martyred spirit has proved the moral grandeur of simple virtue.

You, apparently, feel nothing of this. For you Milly Theale is "a stupid dove," and since husbandry is not your calling, you would prefer a wild pigeon. This is a sentimental prejudice, and to introduce a phallus into the argument does not make it less sentimental. You have a wistful longing for the symbols of antiquity. I love them, too, but in their remote context. Henry James's symbols—and his work is dense with them— are drawn from the confusion of our present way of life, and are all the more vivid for being familiar.

Having said all this, as firmly as I can, I am then will-ing to make substantial concessions to your point of view —no, not to your point of view, because I believe we are standing on separate ground—but I will admit that the view includes a lot of dowdy furniture and a figure that inspires my respect rather than my love (unlike Coleridge, who inspires my love rather than my respect). I had never the slightest desire to meet the author of *The Spoils of Poynton,* and the Son and Brother of the autobiography remains a cold monster of detachment. The style is in keeping with such a character; its baroque opulence hides a suite of small rooms, and the style is doomed to become historical.

I doubt if we can take this argument any further. For me Henry James is the end of a trail, and if I do not read him any longer it is because I do not read fiction any longer. James seems to have taken the art as far as it can go. What comes after James—Joyce, Kafka, Virginia Woolf—seems by comparison a loquacious desuetude. Proust, too, though he is a memorialist rather than a novelist. We shall re-read Proust when we feel nostalgic.

on ROBERT GRAVES
and T. S. ELIOT

## on ROBERT GRAVES *and* T. S. ELIOT: 1

DEAR HERBERT:

I know it is your feeling that we should raise no cenotaph to a noddy. However, we live in the age of gigantic dwarfs, and does it matter whether a mumper of Olympus is a well-known little man or Professor Dead Brains? Ben Jonson ridiculed Dekker in his *Poetaster*, and Dryden rolled Settle in a truss of nettles. Shall we stand by and watch the Tartuffes of the literary stews of the newspapers throw cant and obscurity on helpless books?

Shall we cheat Venal Scribbler of immortality; why his name falls out of my heart, so how could I grudge him a rogue's epitaph? A sluggish tortoise, he never mentions a wit not as dim as his own, or a talented author who has just appeared, for he has never cared to hurry history. As a guerdon for the oblivion he has given genius, he has champagne and pheasants' eggs to douche his gullet. Slow, though sure of his path, he has aided scholarship enormously by discovering *Genesis* in his twelfth lustrum.

The mediocre cannot read the savants without making them smell as much as the waters of the Anigrus which became fetid after Cheiron had washed his wounds in it. Today, the *Iliad* gives off a noisome odour and from the same cause. No book that is sacred to the human race is immune from this plague, for as soon as a dunciad, a goose-cap, a dizzard lays hands on the *Odyssey,* the *Four Gospels, Lear* or *Genesis,* it stinks!

There is Suet Book-Grub who regards every intellect as his personal Nemesis. Authors are no better than asses who feed on wormwood and thistles, and though this is very true, no one is in a better position than Suet Book-Grub to declare it, as he has graved every gifted poem and essay of our time.

There are the monetary priests of our Foundations, better known in our barbaric vernacular as the Chamber of Commerce of the Muses. They reward every ape of the literati who has perfumed his hirsute parts with Mammon. Shrewd rather than noble, they give prodigal awards to the freebooters of literature. They are governed by the screed that every fool is the peer of every sage, which John Ruskin did gainsay, when he claimed that we have relinquished liberty for equality.

The book-reviewing sty is no better. A bawd is a Magdalene at the sacred tomb, and a chit blowing her hindquarters can sound Gabriel's Trump, if Iscariot Reviewer, who betrays a book for two pennies a word, can sink any lower than he is. What is so precious to mortals as a truthful book; according to the Gnostics, the cock crowing at dawn is called the Logos, which is the crier of the *Gospel of St. John.* What then is dawn but Homer and Christ, and are they for sale?

You are familiar with my earnest conviction that we cannot produce a sublime literature without ritual and legends. English is dead, and not even the cormorant or the bat sits upon its Babylonian wastes. No rivers flow through the language, though Homer is said to have composed the *Iliad* by the stream Meles. The teal and the widgeon have disappeared from our books; and every plant and animal, the source of symbols and pure speech, have died in modern literature. English must be put back into the ground to grow again; Sibyl, the child of the Muses, after her interment, sprang up as grass and weeds.

You can imagine my transport when I thought that I had found a mythographer. I had bought *The White Goddess* and *The Nazarene Gospel Restored* by Robert Graves, but soon regretted my folly. The purchase of a bad book is a cruel and humbling debt which costs one a tittle of self-esteem, besides the money. I considered myself unluckier in this instance than poor Chatterton, for when the Lord Mayor of London died, he said, "I am glad he is dead by three pounds, thirteen shillings, and sixpence."

Pedants are birds of prey who never touch English unless it is garbage. The grammarian is always an intellectual corpse, making the most dreary and banal remarks in correct and lifeless sentences. Memory rejects a mediocre style, for Mnemosyne is a goddess of ecstasy which binds together a whole poem. The ancient poet or scholiast knew the whole of the *Iliads* or the *Theogony* of Hesiod, but one would despair of remembering one page by Robert Graves, since he lacks the intellectual passion to assemble the gods within his breast.

In a morose tract on modern authors which Graves calls *The Crowning Privilege,* he offers diverse laws on prosody he has borrowed from the Druids, but his own diction is listless and undisciplined. He could have written just as poor verse without a knowledge of these turgid, druidic laws. Collins was sorely hurt, and cast away all the hopes he had that he was a poet because he had employed the wrong principles for the creation of his pastorals. Graves, a drab of a stylist, is unable to bring homage to the deities. As Horace has remarked, the votary cannot celebrate the gods without taking up the lyre. *The White Goddess* is a loose farrago of blowsy polysyllables which neither quenches the soul nor delights a learned palate. The best style combines frugal words with sublime ones, and can best be described as Ariadne taking her last rest in an earthenware coffin.

All the faults of a bad author can be attributed to sloth; Odysseus must accomplish his fate, but his companions, content with the masts thrown to them by Circe, are "porkers in tears." *The White Goddess* is the labour of other authors: Robert Graves has played the rôle of Hermes, the coney-catcher, and the books he has had his wily fingers in are Smith's *Dictionary of Greek and*

*Roman Biography and Mythology,* published in 1864, and Gerald Massey's *Natural Genesis,* published in 1883.

Graves does his part in comic socks whereas T. S. Eliot wears the tragic buskin. The Olympian cheater has no voice, or a feeble one; the prophetic fountains within our poets are dried up, or as Plutarch has said, the oracle of Tiresias has failed. Poets are great inward angels, which, in the words of Philo Judaeus, signify contemplation; but Isis, Persephone, the Aurora Borealis, and the land of the Hyperboreans can only be discovered by traveling through one's soul.

A dictionary is a book of reference and not the source of erudition; Orpheus, the interpreter of the gods, was said to tame our tigers and lions, but hardly by winnowing his knowledge of Zeus, Artemis, and Set from one lexicon. Hermes of Mallorca has sundry ruses; the most apparent stratagem is to make prodigal acknowledgments to everybody with the exception of those authors whose books he has used most. In short, there is no mention of Smith's remarkable collation of legends and eponymous heroes, or Gerald Massey. Pausanias, Diodorus of Sicily, Plutarch, Philo, and the *Zohar* do not empower *The White Goddess* as Typhon starts the source of the Orontes at the spot where she descended into the earth. Hermes the Sciolist finds the tripod at Delphi of far less use than the index of a mythologist. Though Hermes is not a philologist, a polymath, and cannot distinguish one Egyptian dynasty from another, or an

Hebraist, he feigns to know that the ancient legends of
Britain and the Gaelic tribes derived from the prophet
Ezekiel and the Jewish Rabbins. Hermes is neither a
Kabalist, nor deeply versed in the Jewish apocryphal
works, for six years after the appearance of *The White
Goddess* he collaborated with Joshua Podro who fur-
nished him the Jewish sources for his *Nazarene Gospel
Restored.*

Gerald Massey provided Hermes with the idea that
the Generatrix came first, since woman and not Adam
was the begetter, and that as the understanding of myths
declined the gods were masculinized. This is the theme of
*The White Goddess.* The other stratagem of Hermes is
to purloin a conception of Massey, and then to argue
against it, or clothe it in some reference he has taken
from an author on the Gaelic alphabet.

What is there to comfort a potent mind except myths
and not Dialectic which Hercules set about to abolish
before he freed Prometheus?

It is impious to impugn Plutarch, and he who castigates Herodotus, Milton, and Blake shows the grossest
ingratitude to nature. Buffon honours Aristotle, though
his ornithology is often wrong, and Humboldt has no less
regard for the Stagirite. Besides, Plutarch's *Isis and
Osiris* is enough for any tender intellect though it may
not always be good Egyptology. Suppose Izaak Walton
makes a foolish remark about the habits of fish, or that
in some ways it is as apocryphal as the travels of Sir

John Mandeville, who will deny genius the right to her imperial errors?

There are flaws even in Homer, says Longinus; Thoreau, the greatest American trembler, and I care not a straw for a man who does not shake when he reads the wise, is so content with the *Iliads* he declares that when Homer says the sun has set it is poetry.

Zeus is invariably just, so that it is possible in this life for a dwarf to possess every foible of the Titan. Human wiles are so baffling, that if a man has enough spite, rancor and envy in him, he looks as large in his deformities as Falstaff when he runs his sword through the dead.

## on ROBERT GRAVES *and*
## T. S. ELIOT: 2

DEAR EDWARD:

I think I shall decline the Graves gambit. Partly because I gather from one or two reviews that I have read that he has been attacking me in a recent book—for what cause I know not, and I have no curiosity to find out. But the real reason I cannot write about him is that I have no adequate knowledge of his work. I read his war book when it first came out, and I admired it because it dealt angrily and righteously with an experience that I too had endured. I cannot read his fiction, which he confesses is bread-and-butter work, and I have never had time for his mythological works. As for his poetry, I recognize its cleverness but it never moves me: it is essentially a-musing, a word which has nothing to do with the Muse, but means to stand animal-like with your muzzle in the air. The man has a nose for oddities, idiosyncrasies, for doxies of every kind. A coney-catcher, as you say, self-exiled to a rocky island. I wish him good hunting. He has some honorable scars.

The prophetic fountains within our poets are dried up, but the philosopher Collingwood, who has some good things to say about poetry, gave *The Waste Land* as an example of a work of art that could forego amusement and magic, and find its justification in prophecy. Every community needs its prophet, a man who will utter the secrets of its heart, secrets it dare not utter itself, secrets of guilt and remorse, and above all the speechless fear of death. Evils of ignorance, Collingwood calls them, for which there is no remedy. "The remedy is the poem itself." Art, he concludes, is "the community's medicine for the worst disease of mind, corruption of consciousness."

I am not going to suggest that Eliot himself has an uncorrupted consciousness—he would be the first to disclaim such a state of grace. But he has consistently thought of the poem as a prophylactic, as a purifying agent in human society. At times I have resented his tendency—in theory rather than in practice—to regard art as a moral agency, but that is an old quarrel between ourselves. His image of the catalyst is much safer, for that preserves the integrity of the work of art, its *Schein*, as Schiller called it, its "semblance" as Susanne Langer translates. The work of art is always obstinately itself, a piece of evidence, a real event, a revelation. Naturally it is there to be understood, for communication to take place; but whether we like it or not is irrelevant. Beauty is truth, and truth beauty, but to recognize truth or experience beauty does not necessarily give us pleasure.

The truth conveyed by a Greek tragedy, or by one of Rembrandt's late self-portraits, or by *Les Fleurs du Mal,* is confessional, penitential. But it is also redemptive, purifying. The work of art "works" by virtue of its formal qualities—in the case of poetry, specifically by rhythm. By necessary rhythm, by compulsive rhythm, by a mesmeric inducement of mood and imagery.

It is not my intention to bore you with a theoretical disquisition, but the phenomenon of modern poetry (I call it a phenomenon because it is an apparition, a revolutionary event)—this phenomenon cannot be "evaluated" by college professors. *The Waste Land* has called forth as much critical exegesis as *Paradise Lost,* and it is all unprofitable—no better than Graves's mythologizing. Eliot's worst enemies are his commentators, for they have dug mounds and ditches between the poetry and the public. It is impossible now to read Eliot with an uncorrupted, an innocent mind. I did so read him, forty years ago, and did not stop to ask any questions. There were no learned notes to the first printing of *The Waste Land,* and it now seems to me a pity that the poet ever scattered these clues. It has become the biggest paper chase in the history of criticism, and meanwhile the still small voice of prophecy is drowned by the baying of the hounds.

All art, as Otto Rank has suggested, is an expression of the will to immortality. Negatively, it is an expression of the fear of death. Superficially the poet may hope to overcome death and oblivion by the creation of immortal works, but that is not the deepest sense of the process. In the deepest sense the poet is not "hoping" or acting consciously in any manner, but attaining, by concentration and inward withdrawal, a state of consciousness which—whether it is illusion or not—overflows the bounds of personality, makes contact with racial memories, with group feeling, with what Jung calls the archetypal symbols of the unconscious. I must confess that such hypothetical concepts make me uneasy, but the mechanism of the human brain is complex enough to contain the empirical foundations for them. But admittedly all this is speculation. What is not speculative, but "felt along the nerves," is the physical response of my organism, and surely yours, to the poetry—

> April is the cruellest month, breeding
> Lilacs out of the dead land, mixing
> Memory and desire, stirring
> Dull roots with spring rain . . .

To read those lines, and the 429 lines that follow, *for the first time,* is an authentic and incomparable poetic experience—incomparable, because even the finest lines of Shakespeare or Baudelaire cannot be experienced with the same actuality—the same personal application. Eliot was the prophetic poet of our time, projecting the images of our guilt and remorse, accusing our consciousness of corruption, and recalling us to "the Peace which passeth understanding."

I have never sought to dissolve the unity of that first overwhelming impression. Whether the poem affected me in any deep metaphysical sense I doubt: I was too interested in the created phenomenon, in the creative miracle; for what Eliot had proved, to a younger poet, was that the language could be reanimated; and what the critics even at that time called its Alexandrianism (one of them spoke of "the maggots that breed in the corruption of poetry") was barbaric splendor in my unwearied eyes. Even now, when I am more instructed and therefore less receptive, I read the foxed pages with nostalgic emotion.

Nostalgia! I saw some reference to it lately, berating it as a literary sin. Half the literature in the world is nostalgic, for we seek continually to recover our lost innocence—and this is perhaps the secret of style. Most of our days we think, speak and write in a demotic jargon, the currency of the mob, worn smooth for easy gossip and discourse. To find new currency for new perceptions and thoughts is the task of an uncorrupted consciousness—new metal, new moulds, a fresh minting for each occasion. It is a task demanding more concentration than most of us can command, but we can sometimes by memory recover what I would call first occasions, when events impinge on the consciousness for the first time and for the first time we formulate the appropriate verbal icons. Such events are often far to seek, through thorns and thickets of conventional speech, and when they shine out of the obscurity of the past, we then recognize them with emotion. Such emotion is nostalgic —the return of the prodigal sensibility.

You may accuse me of avoiding the issue by concentrating on one poem of Eliot's but this poem is the *point de repère* for the whole of modern poetry, just as Picasso's *Demoiselles d'Avignon* is the *point de repère* for the whole of modern painting. One can find the origins of Eliot's poetic diction in Elizabethan blank verse or in Laforgue (just as one can find the origins of Picasso's style in African sculpture or the paintings of Cézanne), but at this *point* a fusion takes place, a new symbolic imagery is created, the unknown becomes known.

I have not forgotten Ezra Pound, or Yeats. The time was propitious, there was what Jung calls "a meaningful coincidence in time," what Hippocrates called one common flow, one common breathing, when all things are in sympathy. In the whole civilized world at that time (and I do not exclude Russia, where Mayakovsky, Esenin and Pasternak were active in poetry, Malevich, Kandinsky, Gabo and Pevsner in painting and sculpture) there was such a stirring as Yeats described in his poem on "The Second Coming." We were all on tip-toe at that time, ready to welcome some "vast image out of *Spiritus Mundi.*" By now it seems there has been a miscarriage: the image has been shattered by war and tyranny, and these poets, who should have heralded a Renaissance, are themselves sunk into reaction or apathy, and their works have become thesis fodder for American critics.

It is my faith that eventually our poets will return to that "ceremony of innocence"; otherwise I see no possibility of a revival of poetry or any other art. But my faith grows dim. It is not that things continue to fall apart: on the contrary, there is a consolidation of ignorance, superstition and that ideal of *comfort* which to Burckhardt meant the end of our Western European culture. Writing in March 1873, exactly eighty-six years ago, he prophesied that our art and science (but he did not mean *our* science) would have the greatest difficulty in preventing themselves from sinking into a mere branch of urban money-making. The utmost effort and self-denial will be necessary, he said, if art and science are to remain *creatively* independent in view of the relation in which they stand to the daily press, to cosmopolitan traffic, to world exhibitions. All these menaces have, since Burckhardt's time, increased a thousandfold, and to them we have added deterrents of which he could have had no conception—air traffic, radio and television. The activity of poetry is now reduced to inconceivable insignificance; and to try and woo the indifferent mob, as Eliot has done in his late plays, is a vain effort.

Why do I cling to my little vial of hope? For no rational reason, for no reason beyond the fact that a few fragments of the wisdom of Heraclitus or the poetry of Sappho have survived through ages of darkness and destruction. Traherne was lost and two centuries later recovered. The music of Bach or Vivaldi, the poetry of Donne and Hopkins—by what slender underground shoots they crept through the black soil of oblivion. Poetry will survive, even our poetry will survive. Its "terrible crystal" is indestructible.

You suffer this neglect more than most of your contemporaries, and that is because you do not make the compromises with the armies of ignorance that Eliot has made, that I have made, that most of us make. I don't know anything about the consolations of martyrdom, but when I think of the humility of Blake, or the voluntary sacrifice of Hopkins, or the accepted obscurity of Emily Dickinson, then I realize that these consolations are real. It is the method of Charity, said Sir Thomas Browne, to suffer without reaction; it is the method of the great poet to write in the sure knowledge that a bright image never loses its lustre, though it be buried in the garbage of a doomed civilization.

on T. S. ELIOT
and EZRA POUND

## *on* T. S. ELIOT *and*
## EZRA POUND: 1

DEAR HERBERT:

You told me in New York that T. S. Eliot had been a friend of yours for above forty years. Now before you defend this *mungrell* versifier I must needs cite Sokrates who asserted that truth is more sacred than friendship.

May I repeat, let us not yearn for the books that deceived us when we were chatterboxes of literature, and be like women who, when big with child, think, as Sir Thomas More averred, that pitch and tallow are sweeter than honey.

What a dissembler I would be if I now pretended that I have not made more mistakes about books than you. I take the following from *The Spectator Papers:* "Methought I was transported to a Hill, green, flowery, and of an easie Ascent. Upon the broad Top of it resided squint-eyed *Errour,* and popular *Opinion* with many Heads." Fools die hard, though, as Homer said, they are an unprofitable load to the earth.

Though man is never free of folly and stupidity, one should know bad and pretentious writing, and, if I deal hard with Eliot and make you wince, I owe no debt except to truth, not even to your charitable heart, too often kind to those who pester the streets of Hellas with their rheumy verses.

What we need today is a Topeth, a place that was outside of ancient Jerusalem, for refuse, where carrion volumes can be buried. Let no churl think that I am suggesting that we appoint a new Bowdler; however, it is a desolation that there is no conceivable way of bridling the appetite for garbage.

Who should trouble with these scantlings of poetry? Even to bother about them makes me "sweat for shame," to lean upon Sir Thomas Wyatt's words. Jonathan Swift once remarked: "Now why does Mr. Pope publish his Dulness. The rogues he mawls will die themselves in peace." Yet, who was more involved in controversies than Swift; moreover, human understanding hangs by the thread of Ariadne, and unearned fame is as long-lived as Methuselah. Even when our new Grub Street hackneys no longer pay heed to these old, cruddled boys, there will always be those wights in our "academies of bedlam" who will rush to defend vitiated and deformed learning, affectation, and a rabble of diseased works. Karl Shapiro, the poet, remarks that the intellectual is not particularly intelligent. Have we not forfeited the kingdom of heaven, which is poetry and the imaginative works of the carnal heart, for terminology?

There is a sickness that rages and kills the affections; this terrible infection has been called ignorance; you can cure a man of almost any malady except that. Worse, there are zealous defenders of this disease who imagine that Eliot and Pound are learned, proving only that they ail more than those they attack.

O God, the task is hopeless, but what else can I do but worship the Pleiades and the little rivers that course through the parched spirit—and hope.

When Turgeniev was asked for whom he wrote, he replied: "For my six unknown readers." Renown is a contagion which scribblers easily catch. A good, thewy author seems to be immune from this sickness, and though our spital houses are filled with well-known bad writers who are said never to recover from this dangerous fever, there is a nostrum for this which few have sense enough to take. All one has to do to avoid the pest called fame is to study Homer, Propertius, Longinus, Simonides and John Webster, and he is sure to be unknown. As for myself, I prefer the famine of Otway, and the insanity of Cowper, Collins and Smart to that most mangy of jades, Pegasus, on which Eliot and Pound have ridden to celebrity.

It is folly to exhort those too avid for notoriety to sit in graveyards and study short, humble epitaphs, which are for those who are civil enough to know when they are dead. Edmund Spenser, who died poor and obscure in some tavern, was forthwith buried in Westminster Abbey.

There are honors dear to the feeling heart. Hear the fable of Hien Po who found a piece of jade which he presented to his prince. The latter had it examined and pronounced it false; for which reason Hien Po's left foot was removed. Hien Po gave the next king the same stone, and this time his other foot was amputated. When Hien Po was decrepit and no longer had any expectations from this world, he brought the stone to the third prince, who said that it was jade. Hien Po was offered gifts and titles, which he declined.

Eliot has followed Henry James's footsteps. Like James, he left the land of the Yahoos for the literary "middens and piggeries" of London. What is droll is that Eliot's work is glutted with the phrases of the American guttersnipe. Why leave the United States to be rid of its vulgarities in order to be a bad St. Louis poet abroad? Sokrates preferred taking the hemlock to ostracism, which was considered the worst punishment to a Greek.

Read, without scorifying shame, if you can, the wartime epistles of Henry James. For his services to England Henry James received the Order of Merit, a title also given to T. S. Eliot. But who would not rather wear a poet's crown of nettles and leaves of nightshade than have a title.

Babel, the cult of sameness and the average, is universal. England has just as large an aesthetic mob for famous rubbish as America. One can become well-known in London or in Rapallo in "despight of Pallas," as Sir Philip Sidney testified. A poet earns what he is in this world, which is not likely to ignore a bard of the petit bourgeois, and it is not amiss to add that a little Jew-baiting gives a man a polite varnish in society and is of inestimable help to a poeticule.

When I was in London, and a friend of the late F. S. Flint, a true linguist and the real founder of the Imagist movement in poetry, whom Pound scarcely mentions, he asked me whether I should like to come to a pub where Eliot, you, Flint, and the deceased, gallant Ragg, came to lunch. Flint said to me: "Tom does not like Jews." However, Eliot was gracious and kind, and did all that he could to be of use to me. I blame Eliot for nothing except the books that he has written.

Let it be said, that all of these groundlings, Joyce, Wyndham Lewis, Pound and himself, affected an abhorrence of the Jew because they thought it was a parcel of a long English literary tradition. That they broke the sacred fables of diction and set up Novelty as the Golden Calf of verse is another matter.

However, the dilemma is not anti-Semitism, ignominious as it is. We are concerned with *belles lettres*, though a few allusions to the life are of some niggish worth.

As for Pound's infamies, his treason to his homeland, or his fascism, and that he rejoiced when millions of tormented people were baked in the cruelest kilns of Moloch, I say little. Why attack him as a malefactor of the common weal when it is so easy to overthrow him for his perfidy to literature.

I accuse these men of having betrayed the trust bequeathed to them by Homer, Hesiod, Horace, Theognis,

Heraclitus, Propertius, Martial, Aristotle, Chaucer, Fletcher, John Webster and Shakespeare. I charge them, along with their dead myrmidons, James Joyce and Wyndham Lewis, with having broken the Ten Commandments of the English language.

If one can assert that a man can be more or less than he is, then I declare that they dwarfed their conceptions for a base recognition. Too much ambition makes an inhuman carcass of man. Both Eliot and Pound were mad to be known, and I am sure that Ezra Pound became an epigone of Mussolini to attain the notoriety otherwise denied him. When Mussolini was dictator, Pound went to Milan to give a fascist speech in wretched Italian to a small covey of Americans who only understood English.

When Ezra Pound was an obscurian in Rapallo, it was reported that he sent his death mask to the New York *Times* to see what kind of obituary notice he would receive. He was not mentioned at all. He prates much of *usuria*, but Ethel Moorhead, the Irish editor of an American magazine, the original *This Quarter*, asked him to contribute a poem, and after it was printed he demanded $350 for it. He had so few readers at that time that he could not have asked a publisher for half that amount of money for an entire book.

Shall I go to the spider and the moth for prophecy and savory knowledge? I live in an age in which virtue uneasily billows in the nauseous throat. Why then let old honest Dekker teach me the seven cardinal *sinnes:*

Pack-Penny fathers, covetous rooting moles,

. . . . . . . . . . . .

. . . the *usurer* must behold
His pestilent *flesh*, Whilst all his *gold*
Turns into Tokens, and the *chest*
(They live in,) his infectious breast:
How well heele play the misers part
When all his *coyne* sticks at his heart.

Let us be satisfied, if we can, with philosophy; if, as
Plotinus affirms, whatever is knavish and crass is an
essential ingredient of our lives, then Eliot and Pound
have rewarded those who would sell a birthright for a
miserable pottage of lentils. By the time Ezra Pound
was infamous, the verse that hitherto had been ignored,
except by fools, dizzards, flaneurs, spongers and remit-
tance-men who lounged all day at the Dome or the Select
cafés, now received the noisiest accolades from the
Judas newspapers in America. The newspapers, described by Arthur Symons as the ten plagues of Egypt,
are always giving elite swill to their naïve readers as
though it were the sublime afflatus of the land, while our
truthful books are noticed, if at all, on the back pages
of the public stews for readers. The late Theodore
Dreiser once said to me that what we need is not freedom
of the press, but freedom from it.

The professors are no better and invariably support
the mob taste in arts and letters, or what Allen Tate calls
the "secularization of the swarm." The American wor-
ships the most fell idol in the land, Success, which some-

times goes by the name of pragmatism; or what Allen Tate very eloquently calls "the idolatry of the means."

Eliot is the St. John the Baptist of the vulgar intelligentsia; he, like Pound, sounds the rabble trump for those in the Midian camp of the small aesthetes. They have set back literature a hundred years, and their triumph is the agony and the music of the harper who says to his own soul:

Tell it not in Gath,
Publish it not in Gaza,
Lest the daughters of the Philistines rejoice.

Josephine Herbst, a defiant literary iconoclast in the American wilderness of letters, has said that no one has so corrupted English as Pound. All of our troubles come from the ruin of language. A thief may go to Paradise with Christ, but not a traitor to his own native speech. Eliot, Pound, Joyce and Wyndham Lewis, are matricides, who have slain their mother-tongue.

The Egyptians spoke of their healing libraries: words are the closest symbols there are to the sealed spirit. Good words cure our days, but evil ones make us hoary and decrepit. Whoever harms his own language is born of stocks and stones.

As for these doctors of the neologism, what have we derived from them but a "syntax for old phlegmatic professors," to quote the Goncourts. Samuel Daniel was of the mind that "It is but a fantastic giddiness to forsake

the way of other men, especially where it lies toller-
able." In your own chaste volume, *The Phases of English Poetry*, you quote Dr. Samuel Johnson: "Their wish
was only to say what they hoped had never been said
before."

Both Eliot and Pound are mock Delphic oracles; each
has composed sundry books counseling the raw, sapless
prentices of our new Helicon how to construct an honest
volume. But of what avail is good advice, if the books
themselves are basilisks? Aristotle has asked, what
worth is Gnosis (wisdom) if Praxis (action) be not the
fruit of it? That both Eliot and Pound cite Dante, Villon,
Massinger, Ford, Chapman, Edmund Spenser and Gavin
Douglas, and even use these venerable shades as if they
were their coneys, is bootless; the real hurt comes of
their not having enough force themselves to bray the
Elizabethan quiddities of learning in a mortar, and give
us their own brave conceits. Whatever may be the result of their many ruses, Laforgue, Corbiere and Dante
are what they were before, save that they are no longer
in their own winding-sheets.

It is simple to parody Eliot's literary criticism on a
full stomach or with a lean head, and to compose one of
Pound's *Cantos* while hungry, indifferent or doting.
"Faith, if the truth were known, I was begot after some
gluttonous dinner." The cautelous and chary school-
master's manual on grammar, titled *The Sacred Wood*,
will leave one as thirsty as was Tantalus who could not
reach the water in Erebus.

177

Here is an improvised specimen of Eliot's pursy and sleeveless quibbles; I always have in mind that Eliot, though a meek, faltering man, tries to walk in the buskin:

> I suggest that Shakespeare fell under the influence of Seneca, though Shakespeare, very likely, came to it by cribbing his Seneca from a Latin schoolbook. I do not wish to suggest that the Senecan tragedy came to him through Peele and Kyd. It would be amiss not to know that Seneca himself was a follower of the Greeks. I do not misdoubt that it would be more circumspect to let Seneca sleep in the plays of Chapman and Marston and Ben Jonson. I propose that I am not really concerned with the Roman Stoic in Shakespeare, so much as with Shakespeare's illustration of Seneca's tragedies, though Senecan morals are dull and otiose. We would be immensely ignorant did we not read twelve Elizabethan playwrights at once, which is the only conceivable approach to Middleton's *Changeling*. However, it would be incautious, at least from a late Jacobean point of view, not to know that Middleton did far better descriptions of low life than anything to be found in the comedies of Shakespeare or the satires of Ben Jonson, with the exception of Dekker's chapbooks or Thomas Nashe's *The Unfortunate Traveler*.

Whether Othello, Lear or Iago is less than Shakespeare, whom Mr. Wyndham Lewis regards as a Nihilist, and we have some hint of this from Mr. Noel Coward, I should like to intimate that Webster is not as decadent as Fletcher, and that Tourneur belongs to a period a little earlier than Webster who is closer to Middleton.

Of course, there are two plays which are superior to *'Tis a Pity She's a Whore,* but I do not think this the place or time for such an inquiry. However, Luke Frugal in *The City Madam* is not so great a character as Sir Giles Overreach, but we are in the cemetery of literature, and no one should pass the tombstone of the least of these poets without regarding him as the best he could have been under the circumstances. It is not utterly valueless to asseverate that Queen Elizabeth was parsimonious, and the Countess of Pembroke, sister of Sir Philip Sidney, was doing her uttermost to collate the tergiversations of her age; then, too, the grosser verses of that scullion of the Muses, who wrote *Gammer Gurton's Needle,* are, if not the worst sherd of *folksy* literature we have of that century, at least below the highest.

Some actual museum samples from *The Sacred Sham* are not impertinent after this tender lampoon:

179

I would suggest that none of the plays of Shakespeare has a "meaning," although it would be equally false to say that a play of Shakespeare is meaningless.

. . . the structure of *The Spanish Tragedy* is more dramatic than that of *Arden* or *The Yorkshire Tragedy;* whilst the material of *The Spanish Tragedy*, like that of the other two plays, is quite different from the Senecan material.

If Ford and Shirley and Fletcher represent the decadence, and Webster the last ripeness, then Tourneur belongs a little earlier than Webster. He is nearer to Middleton, and has some affinity to that curious and still underestimated poet, Marston. The difference between his mind and that of Webster is very great. . . .

. . . or to Mr. Havelock Ellis' attempt (in his excellent introduction to the Mermaid volume) to represent Ford as a modern man and psychologist. Mr. Ellis makes the assertion that Ford is nearer to Stendhal and Flaubert than he is to Shakespeare. Ford, nevertheless, depended upon Shakespeare. . . .

What else is there in this, or in Pound's *Selected Essays*, edited by Eliot, except the most fatuous logomachies. Is dullness to be mistaken for the negations of John Dryden?

Eliot, a cairn of spleen, dismisses John Ruskin as a

petulant author of niggard value to our times. What bile
he pours upon the manes of John Donne who he claimed
entered the church for expedient reasons. Donne had
no other way of assuaging his poverty. "After dry breads
and no cake, he washes down his guts with lashings of
water," wrote François Villon. The horses of the Numid-
ians, who never tasted grain, are closer to the Christian
reverence for poverty than is Eliot. Are Eliot's verses,
like Chatterton's, bound together with "clod-agested
reeds?" Does Eliot walk about the earth hoveled in neglect and in the "breme clothes" of Crashaw, Collins or
Christopher Smart? La Bruyère affirmed that "the same
Vices which are deform'd and insupportable in others,
we do not feel in ourselves."

Pound despises John Milton, though the latter's
*Areopagitica* alone has more of the quantity of the heart
in it than all of Pound's refurbished dregs. Eliot has no
patience with Swinburne, but could he have written the
latter's book on Ben Jonson, or could Pound, for that
matter? He snarls at Seneca's essays and Hobbes's
*Leviathan.* T. S. Eliot, putting on his monachal visage,
writes philippics against men of far greater intellect
than his own, as does Ezra Pound. Yet, Eliot himself
asserts that ". . . the search for perfection is a sign of
pettiness."

Herbert, in London we went to St. Paul's and you
showed me the site where John Donne was buried, and
did we not regard the marmoreal sculptured figure of
Donne with those tones of feeling that come from the

harp or the sackbut? I could be more devout by touching the shroud of Donne which he wore for eight years before his demise, than by chafing and fretting my nature with the unthrift reading of *The Sacred Wood*.

I think it is ignoble and a sign of thwarted malice to tread upon the holy ground filled with the remains of the wise. There is malice in all men which, like virtue, can be misused. Give me a gammon of truthful bile, a collop of the soul's rage, without basting it with Christian pietism. Better Villon's honest loathing than Eliot's well-bred venom: "May he howl for four months head downwards in a fishpond, like a bittern. . . ."

It is now recondite literary criticism to praise Dickens and Thackeray, persuading the credulous that grass will grow in those cold regions of Potosi. Dullness is abstruse because the most slavish vice of our century is to be ordinary. A "wappen'd widow" will sooner wed than a mediocre man relinquish his sluttish, feeding days beneath the moon. A hackneyed spirit never so fully reveals himself as when he is endeavoring to be sublime. Apollo was said to have slaughtered the Cyclopes, which are the monsters in men, self-love, vanity, ignorance, and avarice, but there is one beast which no god or mortal can overcome—mediocrity.

"Man is the vulgarian among animals," writes the English author, Olive Moore, and I repeat that Eliot is the St. John the Baptist of the mediocre man coming out of the London drawing-rooms with tea, marmalade and toast.

Call me an inquisitor again, Herbert, but listen to these pitiless commonplaces of Eliot: "Confucius and Buddha are not in the same boat." "If Mr. Forster met Jesus, Buddha, St. Francis . . . I question whether they would strike him as conforming to the ideal of 100 per cent normalcy." His incurable fault is his need to degrade genius. "What Othello seems to be doing in making this speech is *cheering* himself up." "The development of blank verse may be likened to the analysis of that astonishing industrial product coal-tar." On Whitman's 70th birthday Mark Twain congratulated him for having lived in an age when coal tar was invented.

We should inter the true books as Abraham, Isaac, Jacob and Sarah were buried in the Cave of Machpelah, and go there, not to carp at their faults, but to weep for our own.

As for me, genius has no imperfections. Are they to blame because I had no heights, no great Cordilleras within my spirit when I read them? Have I always the same low quantum of the Holy Ghost within me when I study human wisdom? May it not be possible that in some more prophetic season there will be sufficient *energia* for me to absorb more of Massinger, Webster or Ford? It took me thirty years to appreciate that terrible bigot, St. Paul, that Pharisee of the Pharisees. What cormorant ingratitude there is to feed on the words of the sages, as though they were grammatical refuse.

Though I have a blasphemous soul, I would rather befoul the sacred calabash than belittle poor Thomas Chatterton. Was I born to be a scavenger, pecking among the true books that men bleed out of their vitals to teach us that suffering is more human and essential to our miserable understanding than syntax?

Pound, a pedant of the American pleonasm, and one who casts offals upon Thucydides, writes: "Didn't every sane ruler feel that Plato was a faddist?" He is a "cocke of the dunghill of this world," and a steadfast adherent of the grandiose banality: ". . . we feel that Confucius offers a way of life, an Anchauung. . . ." Give a man all the learning there is in the world, and it will not be a covering for his commonplace soul.

The homilies Polonius was supposed to have gleaned from an Elizabethan grammar-book are no less anile than Eliot's remarks on the great Stagirite. Of Aristotle he writes: "He did not have to struggle with German or Italian aesthetics; he did not have to read the (extremely interesting) works of Miss Harrison." Is it not obvious to say that what Miss Harrison learnt about the Greeks and their theogony Aristotle naturally knew? Would it not be as insipid to relate that Homer should have studied Jane Harrison's *Prolegomena to the Study of Greek Religion*, in order to have found out what was in the *Iliads*? Aristotle says, "The spirit, as well as the flesh, grows old."

Of Eliot's nonsense could there be a more fusty example than this divulgation: "I made a careful comparison of the *Medea* and the *Hyppolytus* of Seneca—

perhaps his two best plays—with the *Medea* of Euripides
and the *Phèdre* of Racine respectively; but I do not think
any advantage could be gained by reporting the results
of this inquiry." In the same volume, *The Sacred Wood*,
he adds: ". . . most of our critics are occupied in the
labour of obnubilation."

Having made a great deal of noise in England and
America because he announced that he had joined the
High Church of England, one would expect that Eliot's
own pages would resemble the Ephesian sod and the
verdured, breathing hillocks of the parables of the
Apostles. Where then are the sage thoughts of St. Paul,
Origen, Clement of Alexandria, Eusebius, Tertullian or
Pascal? Can he be so foolish as to offer the reader such
dreary, hymnal trash, in speaking of Lancelot Andrewes,
as this aliment for the paltry doubting Thomases of the
world: ". . . we are completely in the dark as to his
attitude about prayer-book revision."

Is this the posture of low, abject dust? Eliot stoops so
much when he declaims a commonplace that it looks like
an elevated remark. As a pietist he is indigestibly meek,
but who is so bombastic as the humble man? Is hubris a
harder defect in erring flesh than meekness? When Eliot
gives the reader the stalest chaff of one of Bishop Lancelot Andrewes's sermons as a wheaten sheaf from the
Corinthian Epistles, is this the *summum bonum* of cant?

The world can never fill the spirit; the ass may perceive an angel, but Balaam, Eliot, and Pound cannot.

Don Quixote says: "I have been wounded by a phantom," and this was true of Blake who had "the angelic faculty," Allen Tate's phrase.

Why does T. S. Eliot show his sectarian Anglican fangs to Hobbes? We pardon Richard Crashaw, a true religious of poesy, who fell into Doric vacancies in his paean to the sermons of Lancelot Andrewes, because when error is not worldly, it is still a thought with the Nails of the Cross in it.

And what shall one say of Eliot's scorn of Hobbes's plebeian family? Pope's father was a draper, Richard Savage, perhaps, a bastard, and Prior the son of a vintner. "Society," wrote Carlyle, "is founded upon Cloth." Whether it be the cloth of the church or of the world, the material is *Teufelsdrek*. When Hobbes was gravely ill, a shoal of bilious clerics came to his bedside to make him smart the more. Hobbes's reply to them is sufficient answer for Eliot: "Let me alone or else I will detect all your cheats from Aaron to yourselves."

We love and suffer because we are human terrain, hills, ravines, streams, without which we have no bodies. When Ruskin admitted that gneiss in the Alps ceased to be a rapture for him, he knew he had in some way expired. Eliot's one apostrophe is: "Sister, mother and spirit of the river, spirit suffer me not to be of the sea, separated."

He is a disembodied nature; there is almost no locality in him. Doubtless Casanova told many lies, and was impotent when he composed his memoirs; but he at least deteriorated. Eliot sang his senilia when he was young, and he has been a dying swan for fifty years. Eliot's verse has never been virile and for this cause he is land-less; viewing nature with a small, listless eye. Lawrence Sterne wrote: "I pity the man who can travel from Dan to Beersheba, and cry, 'Tis all barren.'"

"The Love Song of J. Alfred Prufrock" is the amour of a disabled male. Osiris is said to have been cut into twenty-six pieces by Typhon, which are the twenty-six letters of the alphabet. Isis recovered every part except his privities, but can a man do his work lacking one letter in his native alphabet? Prufrock is the dead corpus of human speech, a gallimaufry of morsels of Chaucer, Dante, Corbière, Laforgue, Mallarmé, Shakespeare, Poe, Baudelaire, all of which Eliot cannot gather to-gether into a viable, pollened man.

Glutted with American tautologies, insipid ditties and puerile rhymes, both Eliot and Pound are original be-cause they resemble no genuine poet before them. Un-pitying fathers of modern doggerel, who, after Wyatt, Surrey, Gower, Chaucer and Samuel Daniel, but an aca-demic gull or a poetaster, could be deceived by them? But, we have dropped from the constellations to a big dung-heap imagining that we still inhabit Ursa Major.

Impotence is as overpowering a theme as the destruc-tion of seven-gated Thebes. Who scoffs at old age, or jibes at a woman's wrinkles, or sneers at Menelaus, whose phallic force has waned, except the fool who is himself a dotard and a wittol before his days are done. Origen, one of the Ante-nicene fathers, castrated himself, and Abelard was dismembered by enemies, but their works are masculine. Who does not grieve when the summer of his flesh is past? The olive tree suffers from as many diseases as Edmund Spenser who cried out: "All so my lustful leaf is dry and sere." The lament of the licentious Wyf of Bath is nature's tooth in all bodies:

> But age, allas! that al wole envenyme,
> Hath me biraft my beautee and my pith. . . .

However, insipid words give us desponding hours; we are ravaged by verse in ill-health, and our souls are unmanned. It is not Prufrock's chagrins with Aphrodite that withers the tumultuary bones, but the mob verse in which it is divulged. There is no hurt that man or the earth can do to us that is not some advantage provided the words employed in telling it are not feeble. Sir Philip Sidney is our mentor when he reveals:

> Man oft is plagu'd with air, is burnt with fire,
> In water drown't, in earth his burial is;
> And shall we not, therefore, their use desire?

What has Eliot done in any of his doggerel, "The Hollow Men," "The Portrait of a Lady," "Sweeney Agonistes," or "The Hippopotamus," but snivel and pip? Are we so senseless in this grubaean age, to borrow from Swift, as to wallow in such a fatuous ditty:

I grow old, I grow old,
I shall wear the bottoms of my trousers rolled.

Prufrock is a deviscerated Apemantus who loved "few things better than to abhor himself."

Herbert, it is with rueful unwillingness that I even cite such base lines if for no other reason than that I do not wish to lard my days with more stupidity, platitudes and errors than are already mine. I do not go to a book to be more inane and craven than I was before reading it. Here, then, is the lullaby of Eliot's second childhood:

Then how should I begin
To spit out all the butt-ends of my days and ways

And how should I presume?
Is it perfume from a dress
That makes me so digress?

Should I after tea and cakes and ices,
Have the strength to force the moment to its crisis?

And I have seen the moment of my greatness flicker,
And I have seen the eternal Footman hold my coat
and snicker. . . .

To continue with this farrago of puling experiences, and all the same:

And would it have been worth it, after all,
After the cups, the marmalade, the tea.

189

Eliot's complaint is like that of a morbid sutler who has spent his life in a mouldy aerated London restaurant with nothing on his mind but plates and silverware, and who bores you every day with his one tedious refrain: "I have measured out my life with coffee spoons."

Whatever he borrows from others dwindles or is banal when he is done with it. François Villon's recitation is pungent though simple enough:

> . . . we poor . . . fools,
> crouching on our hunkers in a heap, like a bundle
> of old old clothes, over a littel fire of hempstalks.

However, in "The Portrait of a Lady," the palmer-worm has eaten the marrow of the line, and what remains is:

> The worlds revolve like ancient women
> Gathering fuel in vacant lots.

Could Eliot and Pound have absorbed the works of epical shades and made them their own, it would be stupid to denounce them. Ortega y Gasset declared that "the mediocre soul is incapable of transmigration." Longinus has said: "We ought not to regard a good imitation as a theft, but as a beautiful idea of him who undertakes to imitate, by forming himself on the invention and the work of another man." However, to pilfer whole lines from others and lay them next to some ignorant, silly ditty is, to quote John Dryden, to clog the "soil with cockles that opprese the noble seed." Karl

Shapiro writes (*In Defense of Ignorance*): "Eliot's style of deliberate plagiarism is the first symptom of failure to locate the language—in his case a lifelong admission of defeat."

After mangling Dante, Eliot, the advocate of the imperial cliché, which he usually garnishes with a few French, German or Italian words that are supposed to make both Eliot and Pound polymaths, writes:

The corpse you planted last year in your garden,
Has it begun to sprout? Will it bloom this year?
. . . . . . . . . . . . . . . . .
You! hypocrite lecteur!—mon semblable,—mon frère!

What does one make of such rubble and dissociations, buried underneath the vast pile of rubbish in the Mesopotamian Valley like the giant Nimrod, but dig here, who will, and what will you find but:

Madame Sossostris, famous clairvoyante,
Had a bad cold. . . .

or

Oed' und leer das Meer.

Eliot, like Pound, the humbug Gideon of novelties, mawls the old, and calls it new. They either cite Cavalcanti or Marlowe's *Jew of Malta,* or mix English with

191

Italian or French to disarm the reader and appear erudite. Pound, the pseudo-ruffian of letters, has always
stolen the skin of a lion to cover the hide of an ass. "One
law for the ass and the lion is tyrrany," said Blake.

Neither writer is able to be serious or noble without a
smirk. Too coarse to deify either good or evil, *Pulchro
et bono,* as St. Augustine puts it, does not pervade their
words. The common man has not enough strength to be
simple, for there is no sin a man cannot commit and yet
be a poet if he has energy.

Eliot is sublime when he is Chaucer or Spenser, but
as soon as he departs from them he is helplessly himself. Chaucer begins his bracing hymn to Spring:

> Whan that Aprille with his shoures sote
> The droghte of Marche hath perced to the rote,
> And bathed every veyne in swich licour,
> Of which vertu engendred is the flour. . . .

Eliot:

> April is the cruellest month, breeding
> Lilacs out of the dead land, mixing
> Memory and desire, stirring
> Dull roots with spring rain.

Eliot cannot bridle his appetite for the vulgar, and his
deliberate misquotations, a euphemism for thefts, are
invariably followed by villainous commonplaces that
mark our small, warped days, and from which we flee to

poetry. After this rewriting of Chaucer's *Prologue,* Eliot continues:

> . . . we stopped in the colonnade,
> And went on in sunlight, into the Hofgarten,
> And drank coffee, and talked for an hour.

His line after a lovely quotation from Spenser is: "Silk handkerchiefs, cardboard boxes, cigarette ends . . ."

The poet Stanley Burnshaw has said: "Nobody needs to be instructed in the differences . . . between the last six lines of *The Waste Land,* with their six or seven quotations in four languages, and Tennyson's 'Now lies the earth all Danaë to the stars.' " Burnshaw continues: "Take the 74th line of 'Little Gidding.' . . . Readers unfamiliar with 'le tombeau d'Edgar Poe' will assume it to be original Eliot and not a rewriting of Mallarmé: 'To purify the dialect of the tribe' is hardly the same thing as 'Donner un sens plus pur aux mots de la tribu.' "

The reason that Eliot steals the experiences of the French Symbolist poets is that he has so few himself. Who can replenish his soul after a number of pages on toast and tea, a stale London drawing-room, the Thames, or the fish and chip shops of Camden Town, or his perennial, boring fogs. He wears his second-hand verse like a mendicant does his rags.

Both Richard Aldington and Stanley Burnshaw are far more familiar with French poetry than I am. Aldington has stated that Yeats once told him that when Pound was at his best he was somebody else.

Pound pretends that he knows Provençal French, Italian, and Chinese as well as English. Now every ignoramus of our literati palms himself off as a philologist; one publishes a hundred verses from *The Greek Anthology* without knowing any Greek. Ezra Pound procures a Chinese student to explain the *Analects* of Confucius, after which Pound puts it into American grammar to make it new, and there are thousands of dupes prepared for such a hoaxing volume.

Trust no one who babbles too much about his originality. Ptolemy felt he had earned fame for having brought the first jetty, Bactrian camel into Egypt.

Pound is only brand new because he can rob what is old without fear of being detected by those who know even less than he does. But let Richard Aldington take care of this Moll Flanders of the mob intellectuals: Pound's works, relates Aldington, are a "junkshop . . . of spurious artistic curios" filled with "eight verses of Heine, six from the Greek Anthology, while others are translated from Charles d'Orleans, Bertrand de Born, Propertius, du Bellay, Leopardi." Of T. S. Eliot, Richard Aldington says ". . . we have unacknowledged quotations from Edmund Spenser (three times), the Bible, Shakespeare and Paul Verlaine. At the end of *The Waste Land* we have Gerard de Nerval's "Le Prince d'Aquitaine a la Tour Abolie" mixed up with Swinburne and Dante." If my memory does not flag, I believe that Aldington told me Pound also picked the pockets of Meredith, and I do not know how many others.

If I cannot praise Eliot or Pound, it is that I fear by doing so that I am denying the encomia due to another poet.

In *The Waste Land* Eliot takes this majestic, dolorous reflection from the *Inferno:*

> And behind it came so long a train of people,
> That I should never have believed death had undone
>     so many.

Eliot's line goes:

> A crowd flowed over London Bridge, so many,
> I had not thought death had undone so many.

The opening line in Dante's *Inferno* is:

> In the middle of the journey of our life I came
> to myself in a dark wood where the straight way
>     was lost.

which Eliot disembowels:

> Twenty largely wasted . . .
> So here I am, in the middle way, having had twenty
>     years.

In Poe we read: "The venom thou hast poured on me/ Be still, my spirit." But in *Four Quartets* this is the drained line: "I said to my soul, be still, and let the dark come upon you."

Eliot sinks even in lines that are good in another poet: "proffer my deeds to oblivion," which is Eliot's, is a shabby rewording of Odysseus's "Alms for oblivion" in Shakespeare's *Troilus and Cressida*. Lacking passion, the author of *The Waste Land* falls down where Petrarch, in an easy epistolary style, pierces our foreboding grave-clothes; in Eliot it is: "I have lost my sight, smell, hearing, taste and touch . . ."; and Petrarch, in a letter to a friend, has this plaint: "It often seems to me that my throat, my stomach, my tongue, my ears, and my eyes are not part of my body, but pitiless enemies." "Sweeney Agonistes" is a flaccid colloquy in which Sweeney opines that "death is life and life is death," which Eliot has filched from Euripides: "Who knows if life is not death, and death life?"

We are vacant when Eliot wears the prophetic mantle of Isaiah:

> Cry, what shall I cry:
> All flesh is grass.

Following this Eliot is an Isaiah in a double-breasted suit:

> In the land of lobelias and tennis flannels
> The rabbit shall burrow and the thorn revisit,
> The nettle shall flourish on the gravel court. . . .

What else is Eliot in the *Four Quartets* but a spurious Koheleth in *Ecclesiastes*:

And a time for living and for generation
And a time for the wind to break the loosened pane
And to shake the wainscot where the field-mouse
    trots

.  .  .  .  .  .  .  .  .  .  .  .  .  .

The time of the seasons and the constellations
The time of milking and the time of harvest
The time of coupling of man and woman
And that of beasts.

and from *Ecclesiastes:*

And a time to pluck up that which is planted. A
    time to kill,
A time to be born, and a time to die; a time to plant,
And a time to heal . . . A time to weep and a time
    to laugh.

What does Eliot add to Solomon's lament, that the making of many books is a great weariness, when he rephrases it in this manner: "Many are engaged in writing books and printing them . . ."? It is his habit to reiterate the reflections of others while adding nothing of his own: "And they write innumerable books; distracted for silence," is from the choruses from "The Rock." Or when Eliot changes a few words to conceal how he has garbled *Ecclesiasticus:* "Much is your reading, but the word of GOD," and in *Ecclesiasticus* the line reads: "The fear of the Lord, is the beginning of Wisdom." "The poem is a vast paradigm of the possibility of the

Beatific Vision," is from Allen Tate's *The Forlorn Demon.* Who is not moved by Luke's "In the beginning was the Word," or has not found much profit to his spirit in Gnostic speculations about the Logos of Heraclitus, or Logos-Pisces; but what do we gain from these meanderings of Eliot: "The word within a word, unable to speak a word,/Swaddled with darkness. . . ."

What else is T. S. Eliot doing here but imposing upon the ignorance of his readers, assuming that they will never discover his fraud and deceptions, imagining that even if the line is good, it is not to be found either in a far better poem or in a pure, albic page of a saint. What has he done with the parable of creation in *Genesis* except to raven upon it, or add a trite and hollow simile, after which it is a spoiled carcass that even the hungered cannot touch. The following is a humdrum rewriting of *The Book of Ezra* without one radiant perception by Eliot:

> In the days of Nehemiah the Prophet there was
> no exception to the general rule. In Shushan the
> palace, in the month Nisan, And he grieved for
> the broken city, Jerusalem.

There are twelve lines altogether, but let the reader once more turn to *The Old Testament,* and if he has feeling, another word for the learned heart, he will wear sackcloth for the houseless souls who weep for a Jerusalem to cover their heads, as he chants the lamentations of

Ezra. Is it amiss to ask an anti-Semite why he is unable to compose his verses without the help and genius of the Hebrew Prophets?

Eliot and Pound are the two faces of Janus. In "Canto xvi" Pound bawls:

> . . . Blake
> Shouting, whirling arms, the swift limbs,
> Howling against the evil. . . .

In the same pseudo-canto: "Lord Byron/Dead drunk. . . ." Pound also hails Robert Browning as though he were a sodden noddy at the Café du Dome: "Hang it all, Robert Browning,/There is but one 'Sordello!' " Often scatological, Pound probably means Bordello.

Eliot, although more decorous, is as stupid:

> I shall not want Honour in Heaven
> For I shall meet Sir Philip Sidney
> And have talk with Coriolanus
> And other heroes of that kidney.

We live solely to deserve the shrouds of the wise, the noble and the holy sinners. Sokrates shakes every star, leaf and coffin when he says: "What would not a man give if he might converse with Orpheus and Musaeus and Hesiod and Homer?"

Eliot and Pound are emptied of awe, without which the heart is a mouldy fungus that poisons the whole earth. Eliot's longing for the Void is the hatred of the

Six Days of Creation. Does one have to be Minos, in the underworld of the dead, with his Scales of Justice, to tell you that Eliot and Pound weigh nothing?

A mixture of puling, incoherent allusions, an unreasonable mention of names in literature, philosophy and myth is pictorial nihilism. Ezra Pound commits all the errors:

> Falling of the war about the temple of Delphos,
> And of Poseidon, concret Allgemeine,
> And telling of how Plato went to Dionysius of
>     Syracuse.

or elsewhere: "Dido choked up with sobs. . . ." or

> Poor old Homer blind,
> blind as a bat,
> Ear, ear for the sea-surge. . . .

This is repeated, I believe, three times; one with a tender palate for Homer's knowledge of Oceanus, will find the most acute pleasure in Strabo's first volume on the Geography in the *Iliads*. And Pausanias, no thinker or poet, transcends Pound on any page. A random example from Pausanias: ". . . Hesiod in his *Catalogue of Women* says that Iphigenia did not die, but became Hecate by the will of Artemis."

Pound also asserts that the "world like the locust shells . . . [is] moved by no inner being. . . .": it is these fractured references that have no internal value in the

*Cantos* that have been the pitfalls of readers. Pound only appeals to the ear, not to the hearing heart, without any regard for sense, reason or feeling.

More of Pound:

> The camel drivers sit in the turn of the stairs,
> Look down on Ecbatna of plotted streets.

The tumuli of Mordecai and Esther are still to be seen in Ecbatna, the summer palace of the Medic kings, and such precious knowledge should be interred in Ariadne's earthenware casket. In "Canto iv" we have: "The Centaurs heel plants in the earth loam." Followed by this ludicrous inversion: "Came lust of travel on him, or romerva . . ." These lines drool from a maulkin who wipes the words from her chin as though it were foam and spittle: "Came lust of women on him/ And out of England a knight with slow-lifting eyelids. . . ." And in "Canto xiv": "While Menelaus piled up the church at port/ He kept Tynadarida." And: "The dogs leap on Actaeon,/ hither, hither, Actaeon. . . ." It is hard to know whether Ezra Pound is calling the mastiffs or Actaeon, who was their meal. Were we not living, as Samuel Daniel has it, in such *lack-learning times*, what versifier, now canonized by the academic bursars of Minerva, would dare to be such a buffoon?

The laziest of all music is the music of agreeable words that have no genuine function in a poem. Pound writes: "We have heard the faun chiding Proteus/

In the smell of hay under the olive trees. . . ." In "Canto ii": "Had as well listen to Tiresias, and to Cadmus,/ or your luck will go out of you."

Would you not think the following, hackneyed lines, basted with Italian, were Pound's, which are from Eliot's *Four Quartets:*

> Women who have seen their sons or husbands
> Setting forth, and not returning:
> Figlia del duo figlio . . .

Eliot and Pound bait their hearers as though they were angling for mullets; they snare them with a morsel of Dante, a quotation from Marlowe's *The Jew of Malta,* or from St. John of the Cross, or by simply mentioning Agamemnon, Odysseus, Menelaus or Clement of Alexandria; of course, the reader, starved for erudition, and elevated by a great poet or church father, swallows the citation, and is caught. In "Sweeney Agonistes" the verse commences with a marvelous thought from St. John of the Cross:

Hence the soul cannot be possessed of the divine thought, until it has divested itself of the love of created beings.

Then, the poet himself continues:

> Dusty: How about Pereira?
> Doris: What about Pereira?
> I don't care.

> Dusty: You don't care!
> Who pays the rent?

In "Mr. Appollinax" Mr. Eliot quotes a line from Lucian, after which the verse starts:

> When Mr. Appollinax visited the United States
> His laughter tinkled among the teacups.

In the poem with the Italian title, "La Figlia che Piange," Eliot offers us this ineptitude:

> Stand on the highest pavement of the stair—
> Lean on a garden urn—
> Weave, weave the sunlight in your hair. . . .

Eliot, as is evident, is always masking his bathos. The only realities he appears to know are the cheap Joycean ones:

> Sweeney: I know a man once did a girl in
> Any man might do a girl in.

Again he drops into one of Joyce's puns: "A cream of a nightmare dream. . . ."

Pound's *Cantos* are the greatest hoax in the history of literature. The reader is asked to accept, on faith, a muck-heap of allusions, names, legends, that the author is unfamiliar with, and has not himself absorbed. In *Ecclesiasticus* it is written: "All bread is sweet to the whoremonger."

We trust in what we read and this is wise reading, and the only way to learn. As Ignatius Loyola once said: "A pupil is a corpse in the hands of a teacher." A generation of readers have thus heeded Eliot and Pound; if they are fools the reason is that they were deceived, but worse than never being deceived is always to be a gull.

Some may claim that these men wrote some viable sentences, but whose are they? Besides, if a fusty writer blunder into a civil thought, his many baneful conceptions are the stygian reward for spending our miserable brains upon him.

In his *Literary Essays*, edited and selected by Eliot, Pound, mumping Demetrius on style, and slyly lowering the wick of Pallas Athene's lamp, defines phanopoeia, logopoeia, and melopoeia, instead of explaining epiphonema, aposiopseis, or an enthymae. Obviously, Pound can only simulate what he cannot understand, and who gives novices counsel about writing in a scrabbled prose style? Had not Ezra Pound so much influence upon the literary novitiate, the *Cantos* would be a jest, and it is, but in a "house of mourning."

Demetrius states that "The homoeteleuton is used when sentences end in a similar way. They may end with identical words." Tautologies are likely to produce a heavy glubbered sleep, particularly in a long work. Ezra Pound makes much noise, which is false vigor, and has the sound of heavy, snoring matter. Pound's addled misinterpretation of the lesson he learned from Demetrius is:

And because that son of a bitch,
Franz Josef of Austria. . . .
And because that son of a bitch Napoleon Bar-
biche. . . .

Who wagglies it so that Galeaz should sell Pesaro
to Alex and Gossembrone to Feddy;
and hadn't the right to sell.

Bog of stupidities,
malevolent stupidities, and stupidities,

the perverts, the perverters of language,
the perverts. . . .

dead maggots begetting live maggots. . . .

Demetrius points out that "tautology produces stateli-
ness as in Herodotus": "In some places in the Caucasus
huge serpents were found—huge and many."

In "Canto xiv," Pound with latrine humor, that amuses
those musty, wry boys, who never become men, writes
of: ". . . a scrupulously clean table-napkin tucked
under his penis. . . ." Or who has the nostrils to smell
one canto which includes:

Petrified terds . . .
maggots
black beetles, burrowing into the sh-t
flies carrying news, harpies dripping sh-t through
the air . . .

(which brought an Anglican smirk from Dame Sitwell.)

Telling the boys of our new, gimcrack Helicon, to eschew "painted adjectives," like "dim land of peace" which are for "drivelling imbeciles," he offers us the following:

> . . . tin flash in the sun-dazzle.
> pomegranate pale in the moon shaft
> Night of the golden tiger
> The silvery water glazes the upturned nipple
> Sniff and pad-foot of beasts (and repeated)
> I have seen what I have seen . . .

The Greeks, said Horace, received a ready wit and rounded phrases as a gift from the Muse, but Pound assails Thucydides, Virgil, Tacitus, Milton, only to give us the swill of Phlegethon.

Pound is supposed to know a great deal about metre. Do I care for a whole hexameter of stupidity? Why should I trouble with a dullard because he takes the precise number of steps in an iambic when he babbles? Who will bleed at Philippi for the puerile rhymes of T. S. Eliot: "the women come and go/ talking of Michelangelo." It is true that few can endure anything unless it is pocky, little and banal.

Should we cling, as you have told me, Herbert, to our memories; shall we be lotophagi because we are unwilling to relinquish our nostalgic vagaries of the past? No one should love his remembrances more than his life; few will renounce the longing for poverty, a disease or an infernal childhood, because we cannot be young again, but who would care to be as stupid as one was at thirty. I believe it is far easier to translate the water into the wine at Cana than to be intelligent for half an hour. Since I must err, let my sins be mountains, my wickedness be of granite; for I know that whatever knowledge I may claim is as small as the cummin seed.

I beg you, then, because of my admiration for you as a person and a marvelous prose stylist, to break the old memories: "And he who hath to be a creator in good and evil—verily, he hath first to be a destroyer, and break values in pieces."—*Thus Spake Zarathustra*. I have "windmills in my brains," let it be so. Plotinus himself is said to have achieved a vision of the Absolute four times. That there are no Absolutes is of no importance; but he who refuses to strive after them is a liar, a coward and a caitiff.

There is much noise about blustering syntax being good because it represents our times. Do I wish to be the vessel of every fatuity, scab, murrain or filth to prove to dizzards that I know my century? I prefer to die an anachronism than to be a famous simpleton of the twentieth century. There are no heteroclites of letters, for who can avoid the hellebore we call the world? Soon as I step across the threshold of my frugal apartment, I reflect the imbecility of my era. The shibboleth of the day is that hackneyed words represent our times and that we can become the erudite guttersnipes of Parnassus by committing to paper the remarks of buffoons and addlepates; we are expected to bless famine, idiocy and bad grammar solely to prove that we are alive.

Eliot is not noble, and even after he has culled a piercing line from the *Inferno*, he expires in a banter. Pound, a Polonius gone mad, is a pedant of the American vernacular. Eliot employs servile words because he cannot use towering ones. Dryden said: "One would think, unlock the door, was a thing as vulgar as could be spoken; and yet Seneca could make it sound high and lofty in his Latin."

## on T. S. ELIOT *and*
## EZRA POUND: 2

DEAR EDWARD:

It is not my wish to temper criticism with kind-
ness, but I have always held that sympathy is the beginning of understanding, in literature as in life. Your
attack on Eliot and Pound is, I know, inspired by a
passion for the truth, and if truth is indeed more sacred
than friendship, then I must put all friendly feelings
aside and answer you on your chosen ground. But I am
not quite sure that I agree with Socrates—not, at least,
in the abbreviated form you cite him. Friendship is also
an aspect of truth, and love, as Plato's Diotima said,
stands half way between ignorance and wisdom. One of
the most melancholy aspects of our time has been the
ease with which men have sacrificed their friends for
some "truth," religious or political. I have no intention
of doing that, on this or any other occasion.

It is true that Eliot has been my friend for more than
forty years—there can be few instances in literature of
such a sustained friendship. I would not say that our
friendship has been "easy"—we are divided by serious differences of belief (or unbelief), of moral and

209

aesthetic sensibility. But in so far as we have been poets and critics, we have shared a common background here in England, fought side by side (sometimes face to face), and known about each other's intellectual activities with as much intimacy as two essentially reserved men can accomplish. Let me say at once, therefore, that I can find no correspondence between the man I know and the "apostle of the average" you hold up for our contempt.

Your attack is agitated and random in its thrusts. You nowhere come to grips with any principle, of traditionalism or of faith, that Eliot may be said to represent—if you had, I might have found some grounds for agreement. Your charge, in so far as it is factual and not merely vituperative, is directed to certain *stylistic* features of his work: features which he shares with Pound, and which are, indeed, general characteristics of the art of our time. These features are known as *fragmentation* and *eclecticism*, and they are but two aspects of the same historical development. The charges which you bring against Eliot and Pound could with the same doubtful cogency be brought against Joyce and Faulkner, Picasso and Klee, Stravinsky and Bartok—indeed, against every representative artist of the past fifty years.

I do not intend to defend the age—I am a fatalist and believe that what has happened in the art of our time had to happen, as a logical reflection of what was at the same time happening in society at large. If you object to the fragmentation and eclecticism of modern art, then like

the egregious Sedlmayr you must go back to the origins
of romanticism in the 18th century for your quarry. I
am not preaching some brand of historicism—I do not
believe in such figments as the spirit of the age, or even
the Freudian death-wish; but the simple truth is that man
(including the artist) is moulded by circumstance, and
any attempt to break the mould is merely kicking against
the pricks.

Hence Eliot's respect for tradition—a tradition continuously prolonged and modified by the historical
process—the physical, environmental changes of social
structure. Eliot maintains that he is a classicist: I have
argued (in *The True Voice of Feeling*) that he is a
romanticist paying lip-service to the concept of classi-
cism. In any case, the label is not important: he is a man
of his age, a fact which gives him his significance.

What I (and others) call fragmentation in art is a
process due to the cracking of the mirror of illusion: the
deliberate breaking of the unity of the reflected image
that used to be called reality. A poet like Dante (whom
you quote) or Wordsworth (in *The Prelude*) is trying
to create an image of wholeness: the art of the past (or
classical art) is an attempt to impose unity on the multi-
plicity of sense impressions. The modern artist (poet,
painter or musician) is convinced that such imposed
unity is false—simply not true. Reality has only one
possible center of coherence: the individual consciousness, and that is not a permanent and persisting focus:
we are only conscious when we are conscious of some-

thing. The only unity we can achieve is constituted by the bridges we hastily improvise between one sense-impression and another, and poetry is the bridge with the widest span (science is an attempt to coordinate or connect a maximum number of sense impressions, which art wishes to keep vivid and discrete).

You may think such generalizations avoid the immediate issue of Eliot's poetry, but if you will now re-read *The Waste Land* with them in mind, I think you will find it makes a difference. *The Waste Land* is a uniquely significant poem because it accepts this new conception of reality (i.e., of immediate experience) and in remaining true to the fragmentary or disjointed nature of our consciousness, presents an image of reality far more acceptable to the disillusioned mind of modern man.

The same justification can be advanced for any typical product of contemporary art; for *Ulysses*, the *Cantos*, for futurism, cubism and surrealism. They are all fragments of a mirror forever broken; you would need a new spiritual furnace to fuse them together again; and of that, as you would be the first to admit, there is no sign in our age of alienation.

Some of the charges you bring against Eliot and Pound are more personal—that they have been vain, ambitious, astute. Some of these accusations may be true, but they are on a level of personal criticism which is largely irrelevant. Can we be sure that Homer or Shakespeare were good men, or shall we not rather have regard to the advice of Lord Acton and, realizing that good and evil lie close together, refuse to seek artistic unity in a man's character. Your only serious and practical charge is that these men have broken the sacred tablets of the English language, and of this you offer as evidence some sentences detached from their writings. In so far as your citations are from prose works they may be just; "fragmentation" is not an excuse for bad writing. But critical argument is rarely maintained with logical or stylistic consistency. I can think of only Aristotle's *Poetics* and Shelley's *Defence of Poetry* as perfect prose patterns, devoid of quibbles and irrelevancies. You may add Longinus, if you wish, and perhaps the essays of Dryden. But think of the meandering formlessness, a stream that continuously loses itself in quibbling sands and bogs of irrelevancy, that is Coleridge's *Biographia Literaria*. And that is the most seminal work of criticism in our language; *The Sacred Wood* is by comparison a place of light, where one can wander without fear of getting lost.

Against your museum samples of "grandiose banality" I must bring some refuting evidence. There are many passages in *The Sacred Wood* or the *Elizabethan Essays* that have become focal points in the development of modern literary criticism. I will not quote one of these because I believe they have usually been misused by academic pedants, prowling for some morsel of obscurity to bury under their fatuous exegesis; and I know that Eliot himself regrets having given currency to such provocative slogans. Here, by contrast, is a passage as human and as perceptive and as beautifully expatiated as anything in Dryden or Coleridge. It is concerned with Goethe, but maybe it has some present application:

> In the development of taste and critical judgement in literature—a part or an aspect of the total process of coming to maturity—there are, according to my own experience, three important phases. In adolescence, I was swept with enthusiasm for one author after another, to whichever responded to the instinctive needs at my stage of development. At this enthusiastic stage the critical faculty is hardly awake, for there is no comparison of one author with another, no full awareness of the basis of the relationship between oneself and the author in whose work one is engrossed. Not only is there but little awareness of rank; there is no true understanding of greatness. This is a standard inaccessible to the immature mind: at that stage, there are only the writers by whom one is carried away and those who leave one cold. As one's reading is extended, and one becomes acquainted with an increasing variety of the best writers of prose and verse, at the same time acquiring greater experience of the world and stronger powers of reflection, one's taste becomes more comprehensive, one's passions calmer and one's understanding more profound. At this stage, we begin to develop that

critical ability, that power of self-criticism, without which the poet will do no more than repeat himself to the end of his life. Yet, though we may at this stage enjoy, understand and appreciate an indefinite variety of artistic and philosophic genius, there will remain obstinate cases of authors of high rank whom we continue to find antipathetic. So the third stage of development— of maturation so far as that process can be represented by the history of our reading and study —is that at which we begin to enquire into the reasons for our failure to enjoy what has been found delightful by men, perhaps many generations of men, as well qualified or better qualified for appreciation than ourselves. In trying to understand why one has failed to appreciate rightly a particular author, one is seeking for light, not only about that author, but about oneself. The study of authors whose work one fails to enjoy can thus be a very valuable exercise, though it is one to which common sense imposes limits: for nobody has the time to study the work of all the great authors in whose work he takes no pleasure. This process of examination is not an effort to enjoy what one has failed to enjoy: it is an effort to understand that work, and to understand oneself in relation to it. The enjoyment will come, if it does come, only as a consequence of the understanding."

(*On Poetry and Poets*)

Your charges against Eliot's verse ignore whatever
defense may be made of fragmentation or eclecticism.
As for eclecticism, I do not propose to justify it, partly
because I would agree that it can be a tiresome affectation and partly because it is common to all sophisticated
poets—is there not a whole industry devoted to the allusions and pilferings of Shakespeare? At its worst eclecticism is a sign of a weak imaginative faculty, for which
a good memory is some compensation; but at its best it
can represent a fraternity of the craft, and acknowledg-
ment that other poets' images are virtuous currency.

Granted a justification for fragmentation and for the
borrowing of a few rare plumes from Juno's peacock,
there must remain, as a separate and magical achievement, some verse of the poet's own making. Before quoting my own selections to refute yours, I must make quite
clear that I do not for one moment accept your thematic
criterion. "The Love Song of Alfred J. Prufrock" may
be the armour of a disabled male and in his early verse
Eliot does indeed regard nature and man with sterile dis-
gust. But from what other point of view did great poets
like Swift and Baudelaire regard nature and man? Is
your favorite Villon a poet of innocent delight? Martial?
Catullus? No, Edward, we have argued this point before
in our correspondence, and I cannot allow you once
more to introduce, without challenge, such irrelevant
criteria. No censorship can be imposed on the imagination, and the truth we should hold sacred (and perhaps
Socrates meant this) is truth to the divine promptings of

the Muse—promptings which may take the poet into a lady's bedroom or a brothel as easily and as frequently as into the vernal woods or the market place. I believe that every great poet has *nevertheless* a sense of glory; but glory, as we know from the *Golden Legend* and the *Morte D'Arthur*, often shines forth from humble places.

The touchstone of poetry, as all good critics have recognized, is an unanalyzable magic. One line, as Arnold recognized, is sufficient to reveal a poet's authenticity, his uniqueness. You quote with mockery lines like:

> The worlds revolve like ancient women
> Gathering fuel in vacant lots.

The image may be borrowed from a translation of Villon, though I doubt it: but the metaphor, which is more than the image, does not exist in the lines you quote. The magic comes from the constatation of two images: the worlds revolving in infinite space and the ancient women revolving in the finite space of a vacant lot. It is not an easy metaphor, but it seems to me to be an effective one.

Similarly the deliberate imitation of Chaucer's verses in the opening lines of *The Waste Land* is an intensification of the image (and an extension of it), bringing personal poignancy (memory and desire) into a situation where Chaucer found only an abstract virtue.

These are perhaps pedantic points. You will now ex-

pect me to quote lines of pure poetry to match your base
ones, but though a line like

A lonely cab-horse steams and stamps

is pure enough for me, evoking images of an experienced
past, I shall decline the challenge, simply because this
kind of poetry, in spite of its fragmentary nature (indeed because of its fragmentary nature) is not to be
dismembered. The poem is a mosaic, and each tessera,
though it may have its radiance, is rough but irregular,
and only makes sense in the complete pattern. The modern poem is not syntactical, is not even logical or conse-
quential: it is ambiguous, it is complex, it is static—or
perhaps I should say *constatic*, if such a word exists, for
it gets its effect by fusing together what is "more distant
than the stars and nearer than the eye." All things relevant to the mood or the sensation, all images present to
the poet's consciousness, are "by this grace dissolved in
place."

The same principle must be applied to the defense of
Ezra Pound, but in his case fragmentation, as a stylistic
mannerism, has become a process of mental incoherence.
I do not know the exact nature of the psychiatric evi-
dence that was put forward in defense or explanation of
Pound's war-time aberrations, but this is not important.
As the case of Hölderlin shows, the creative impulse can

survive the incidence of schizophrenia, and in so far as
the affliction removes the barriers to the realm of the
unconscious, may bring a new afflatus to a pre-existing
talent. I don't think it has had that effect in the case of
Pound: there has been a progressive increase in incoherence, over many years, and the point has long since
been passed at which an aesthetic justification is possible. But the vatic voice is still there, even in the last
lines of the last canto to be published:

form is cut in the lute's neck, tone is from the bowl

Pound I see as a tragic figure, deserving our pity and
not our condemnation. Nothing can be perfect in our
fragmentary age, but either my senses are dimmed and
my judgment void, or the first thirty *Cantos* concentrate
in their essence a living poetry, rooted in some waste
land of romantic dissolution, but thrusting flowering
shoots into a clear air.

Again, as in Eliot's case, quotation is not to the point
—the gold and purple tesserae need their aggregation,
their multitudinous setting. Detachable images, lyrical
cadences abound, but it gives a false impression to quote
them. Each canto is a *Merzbild,* as Schwitters called his
pictures, and each element in the composition may be a
piece of trash, a bill of lading, a scrap of Greek or Italian, a prayer, an imprecation, a row of statistics, a Chinese edict, a letter from Jefferson—nothing from the
seething cauldron of memory is excluded.

Sawdust rodomontade? Junkshop of spurious artistic curios? These are easy insults, and could be brought against Chaucer or Spenser as easily as against Eliot and Pound. Spenser is one of the greatest of our poets and his *Shepherd's Calendar* a turning point not only for Elizabethan poetry, but for the whole future of English poetry. And yet no one is more dependent on his predecessors than Spenser; his debts to Tasso in *The Faerie Queene* are as great as Eliot's or Pound's to their predecessors. Your objections to Eliot and Pound are, indeed, the same as Ben Jonson's to Spenser, of whom he said that in affecting the ancients he "writ no language." But Ben added "Yet I would have him read for his matter."

I will not insist on Eliot's or Pound's "matter," though it is relevant to the argument; yet I would hazard that in a hundred years' time Pound's obsession with monetary policy may seem to have been more prophetic than eccentric. Both Eliot and Pound have been concerned with great public issues, and you cannot charge them with shallowness. But that is not the difference between us. You are rightly concerned for the integrity of the language, and it is precisely on that point that I challenge you. From their beginnings both poets have been primarily concerned for the word, for the image, for the purification of our poetic idiom. Their revolt was no less a revolt; and although, especially in Pound's case, the revolt has its grotesque moments, and batters away like an army of Sicilian puppets, nevertheless the poetic idiom was cleansed of its grosser accretions, and even a Yeats was brought to the new discipline.

There my defense must rest. Throughout this correspondence, though standing on a common ground, we have been divided by the angle of our vision. You look upward and backward, to your beloved masters, Homer, Hesiod, Horace, Chaucer and Shakespeare. By comparison our modern poets seem puny, pretentious, inarticulate. I am not so ambitious for my age. My vision is horizontal, even cast on the ground we tread on. I see men struggling with immediate evils (the corruption of poetry, the worship of the bitch-goddess, money). The poetry must be written in the mêlée—painting, as Picasso has said, is a political weapon. Homer and Shakespeare, in such circumstances, may seem remote and irrelevant—at least, not imitable in our actions, which are governed by necessity. (But let it be understood, I don't mean political necessity in the Leninist sense: I mean the necessity of enduring our historical situation.) I am not seeking an excuse in opportunism. I know that the values of art are absolute, and that many bubble reputations of our time will be blown away by the winds of destiny. We are all placed in an ambiguous perspective, and must be conscious of our insecurity. But Shakespeare, despite his boastful sonnets, expressed the same doubt and only bad poets are self-confident. We cannot anticipate history—that is my main point—and your invective is in vain. I would prefer to be a modest and uncertain *laudator temporis acti,* content to elucidate where there is darkness, and to imitate in our human affairs the method of reasoning that Cusanus applied to divine things. We should seek a simplicity in which all contradictions are reconciled, and I hold it for the simple truth that the poet, as Shakespeare said, is and should be the interpreter of his time. Works such as *The Waste Land* and the *Cantos,* though they may be no more than symbols of our spiritual impotency, could not be the product of any age other than ours. You speak of the learned ignorance that these works exhibit. I do not know if you had Nicolas Cusanus in mind, but he would have said that your search for the absolute is vain. The absolute truth is beyond our reach, the quiddity of things unattainable, and we, who throughout this correspondence have sought for the quiddity of good writing, had better end by confessing our ignorance.

*Acknowledgments are made to Robert Creeley, Bernard Wall and Monroe K. Spears for extracts which appeared in* The Black Mountain Review, The Twentieth Century *and* The Sewanee Review.